UNTIL THE END OF TIME

Revealing the Future of Humankind

A Study of Daniel and Revelation

Jack W. Hayford

with

Gary Curtis

THOMAS NELSON PUBLISHERS

Nashville • Atlanta • London • Vancouver

DEDICATION

This, the third series of *Spirit-Filled Life
Bible Study Guides,* is dedicated to the
memory of

Dr. Roy H. Hicks, Jr.
(1944–1994)

one of God's "men for all seasons,"
faithful in the Word, mighty in the Spirit,
leading multitudes into the love of God
and the worship of His Son, Jesus Christ.

Unto Christ's glory and in Roy's memory,
we will continue to sing:

Praise the Name of Jesus,
Praise the Name of Jesus,
He's my Rock, He's my Fortress,
He's my Deliverer, in Him will I trust.
Praise the Name of Jesus.

Words by Roy Hicks, Jr., © 1976 Latter Rain Music. All rights administered by The Sparrow Corp.
All Rights Reserved. Used by Permission.

**Until the End of Time: Revealing the
Future of Humankind**
Copyright © 1994 by Jack W. Hayford

Published in Nashville, Tennessee, by Thomas Nelson, Inc.

Unless otherwise indicated, Scripture quotations are from the
New King James Version of the Bible, © 1979, 1980, 1982,
Thomas Nelson, Inc., Publishers

Printed in the United States of America
3 4 5 6 7 8 — 00 99 98 97 96 95

CONTENTS

In Appreciation

This study in Daniel and Revelation is, in part, a tribute to the ministry of Dr. Charles L. Hollis, who, as pastor—for over 45 years—of the historic Gospel Temple in Moline, Illinois, first instilled in the writer an awe and appreciation for biblical prophecy and its modern fulfillment.

About the Executive Editor

JACK W. HAYFORD, noted pastor, teacher, writer, and composer, is the Executive Editor of the complete series, working with the publisher in the conceiving and developing of each of the books.

Dr. Hayford is Senior Pastor of The Church On The Way, the First Foursquare Church of Van Nuys, California. He and his wife, Anna, have four married children, all of whom are active in either pastoral ministry or vital church life. As General Editor of the *Spirit-Filled Life Bible,* Pastor Hayford led a four-year project, which has resulted in the availability of one of today's most practical and popular study Bibles. He is author of more than twenty books, including *A Passion for Fullness, The Beauty of Spiritual Language, Rebuilding the Real You,* and *Prayer Is Invading the Impossible.* His musical compositions number over four hundred songs, including the widely sung "Majesty."

About the Writer

GARY CURTIS is the Executive Director of Living Way Ministries, the broadcast/media ministry of The Church On The Way in Van Nuys, California. He administers an outreach that both daily (radio) and weekly (television) is aired on more than 500 broadcast facilities. His experience as a gifted administrator and pastor has been gained through his involvement in public ministry for over twenty-five years, having served at Illinois' great Moline Gospel Temple with Dr. Charles Hollis and at LIFE Bible College in Los Angeles as Executive Assistant to the President.

He is a graduate of LIFE Bible College, where he was also Student Body President. Graduate studies have been undertaken at Fuller Theological Seminary (Pasadena), at Wheaton Graduate School of Theology, and at Trinity Evangelical Divinity School in Illinois.

Gary and Alisa Curtis have been married for nearly thirty years and have two adult daughters, Carmen and Coleen, both of whom are active in ministry.

Of this contributor, the Executive Editor has remarked: "I know of no one with a steadier, more reliable pattern of service to Christ than Gary Curtis. His trustworthiness and efficiency bring a quality of depth and integrity to everything he does, whether in the study of the Word or his overseeing of demanding administrative detail."

THE GIFT
THAT KEEPS ON GIVING

Who doesn't like presents? Whether they come wrapped in colorful paper and beautiful bows, or brown paper bags closed and tied at the top with old shoestring. Kids and adults of all ages love getting and opening presents.

But even this moment of surprise and pleasure can be marked by dread and fear. All it takes is for these words to appear: "Assembly Required. Instructions Enclosed." How we hate these words! They taunt us, tease us, beckon us to try to challenge them, all the while knowing that they have the upper hand. If we don't understand the instructions, or if we ignore them and try to put the gift together ourselves, more than likely we'll only assemble frustration and anger. What we felt about our great gift—all the joy, anticipation, and wonder—will vanish. And they will never return, at least not to that pristine state they had before we realized that *we* had to assemble our present with instructions *no consumer* will ever understand.

One of the most precious gifts God has given us is His Word, the Bible. Wrapped in the glory and sacrifice of His Son and delivered by the power and ministry of His Spirit, it is a treasured gift—one the family of God has preserved and protected for centuries as a family heirloom. It promises that it is the gift that keeps on giving, because the Giver it reveals is inexhaustible in His love and grace.

Tragically, though, fewer and fewer people, even those who number themselves among God's everlasting family, are opening this gift and seeking to understand what it's all about and how to use it. They often feel intimidated by it. It requires some assembly, and its instructions are hard to comprehend sometimes. How does the Bible fit together anyway? What does Genesis have to do with Revelation? Who are Abraham and Moses, and what is their relationship to Jesus and Paul? And what about the works of the Law and the works of faith? What are they all about, and how do they fit together, if at all?

And what does this ancient Book have to say to us who are looking toward the twenty-first century? Will taking the time and energy to understand its instructions and to fit it all together really help you and me? Will it help us better understand who we are, what the future holds, how we can better live here and now? Will it really help us in our personal relationships, in our marriages and families, in our jobs? Can it give us more than just advice on how to handle crises? the death of a loved one? the financial fallout of losing a job? catastrophic illness? betrayal by a friend? the seduction of our values? the abuses of the heart and soul? Will it allay our fears and calm our restlessness and heal our wounds? Can it really get us in touch with the same power that gave birth to the universe? that parted the Red Sea? that raised Jesus from the stranglehold of the grave? Can we really find unconditional love, total forgiveness, and genuine healing in its pages?

Yes. Yes. Without a shred of doubt.

The *Spirit-Filled Life Bible Discovery Guide* series is designed to help you unwrap, assemble, and enjoy all God has for you in the pages of Scripture. It will focus your time and energy on the books of the Bible, the people and places they describe, and the themes and life applications that flow thick from its pages like honey oozing from a beehive.

So you can get the most out of God's Word, this series has a number of helpful features. Each study guide has no more than fourteen lessons, each arranged so you can plumb the depths or skim the surface, depending on your needs and interests.

The study guides also contain six major sections, each marked by a symbol and heading for easy identification.

 WORD WEALTH

The WORD WEALTH feature provides important definitions of key terms.

BEHIND THE SCENES

BEHIND THE SCENES supplies information about cultural beliefs and practices, doctrinal disputes, business trades, and the like, that illuminate Bible passages and teachings.

 ### AT A GLANCE

The AT A GLANCE feature uses maps and charts to identify places and simplify themes or positions.

 ### BIBLE EXTRA

Because this study guide focuses on a book of the Bible, you will find a BIBLE EXTRA feature that guides you into Bible dictionaries, Bible encyclopedias, and other resources that will enable you to glean more from the Bible's wealth if you want something extra.

 ### PROBING THE DEPTHS

Another feature, PROBING THE DEPTHS, will explain controversial issues raised by particular lessons and cite Bible passages and other sources to which you can turn to help you come to your own conclusions.

 ### FAITH ALIVE

Finally, each lesson contains a FAITH ALIVE feature. Here the focus is, So what? Given what the Bible says, what does it mean for my life? How can it impact my day-to-day needs, hurts, relationships, concerns, and whatever else is important to me? FAITH ALIVE will help you see and apply the practical relevance of God's literary gift.

As you'll see, these guides supply space for you to answer the study and life-application questions and exercises. You may, however, want to record all your answers, or just the overflow from your study or application, in a separate notebook or journal. This would be especially helpful if you think you'll dig into the BIBLE EXTRA features. Because the exercises in this feature are optional and can be expanded as far as you want to take them, we have not allowed writing space for them in this study guide. So you may want to have a notebook or journal handy for recording your discoveries while working through to this feature's riches.

The Bible study method used in this series revolves around four basic steps: observation, interpretation, correlation, and application. Observation answers the question, What does the text say? Interpretation deals with, What does the text mean?—not with what it means to you or me, but what it meant to its original readers. Correlation asks, What light do other Scripture passages shed on this text? And application, the goal of Bible study, poses the question, How should my life change in response to the Holy Spirit's teaching of this text?

If you have used a Bible much before, you know that it comes in a variety of translations and paraphrases. Although you can use any of them with profit as you work through the *Spirit-Filled Life Bible Discovery Guide* series, when Bible passages or words are cited, you will find they are from the *New King James Version* of the Bible. Using this translation with this series will make your study easier, but it's certainly not necessary.

The only resources you need to complete and apply these study guides are a heart and mind open to the Holy Spirit, a prayerful attitude, and a pencil and a Bible. Of course, you may draw upon other sources, such as commentaries, dictionaries, encyclopedias, atlases, and concordances, and you'll even find some optional exercises that will guide you into these sources. But these are extras, not necessities. These study guides are comprehensive enough to give you all you need to gain a good, basic understanding of the Bible book being covered and how you can apply its themes and counsel to your life.

A word of warning, though. By itself, Bible study will not transform your life. It will not give you power, peace, joy, comfort, hope, and a number of other gifts God longs for you to unwrap and enjoy. Through Bible study, you will grow in your understanding of the Lord, His kingdom and your place in it, and those things are essential. But you need more. You need to rely on the Holy Spirit to guide your study and your application of the Bible's truths. He, Jesus promised, was sent to teach us "all things" (John 14:26; cf. 1 Cor. 2:13). So as you use this series to guide you through Scripture, bathe your study time in prayer, asking the Spirit of God to illuminate the text, enlighten your mind, humble your will, and comfort your heart. He will never let you down.

My prayer and goal for you is that as you unwrap and begin to explore God's Book for living His way, the Holy Spirit will fill every fiber of your being with the joy and power God longs to give all His children. So read on. Be diligent. Stay open and submissive to Him. You will not be disappointed. He promises you!

Lesson 1/Approaching Prophecy

You can't buy food at most markets without coming face to face with pop prophecy—tabloid predictions of the weird, bizarre, and ridiculous.

Why do people buy that stuff?

It's because mankind seems to have an insatiable interest in future and unusual events. Consequently, many are the gullible guests of charlatans who dish out truth and error in palatable proportions, preying on unsuspecting souls. Furthermore, some people are deliberately or demonically deceived.

Biblical prophecy is not like that. Its predictions are not only reliable, but divinely inspired: "Knowing this first, that no prophecy of Scripture is of any private interpretation, for prophecy never came by the will of man, but holy men of God spoke as they were moved by the Holy Spirit" (2 Pet. 1:20, 21); "All Scripture is given by inspiration of God, and is profitable for doctrine, for reproof, for correction, for instruction in righteousness, that the man of God may be complete, thoroughly equipped for every good work" (2 Tim. 3:16, 17).

In contrast to the guesswork of human predictions, there are at least four bona fide tests for biblical prophecy:

1. it must be spoken before the event takes place;
2. it must contain a certain number of details to exclude guesswork;
3. there must be a sufficient lapse of time between the prediction and the fulfillment to affirm the facts; and
4. there must be an unveiling of the future which excludes mere human foresight.

As we approach the "end time" and fulfillment of "last days" prophecies in Daniel and Revelation, we see important similarities, symmetry, and sequence. Looking through their eyes, we can see history in advance. We learn of world empires rising and falling and of God's coming kingdom. We glimpse world politics and church-state intrigue. We wonder at the efforts of evil at work in the earth, but rejoice as we see God's spiritual forces overruling world affairs with His righteousness.

 FAITH ALIVE

How is true biblical prophecy distinguished from tabloid-type predictions you may read in grocery store checkout lines?

Someone has described an insatiable curiosity for knowing or sharing some "new thing" as "Athenianism." (See Acts 17:16–21.) What was Paul's experience with this practice?

How do you feel about preachers who may use the study of biblical prophecy as a "drawing device" to get people to come to church or special meetings? Why?

How did Peter use prophecy as a tool to attract unbelievers in Acts 3:12–26? What was the result? (See Acts 4:4.)

How do you feel about people or churches who make prophecy, or a common system of interpretation of prophecy, the basis for Christian fellowship?

Some people object to the study of prophecy. They say it is unprofitable, leading men and women to become dreamers. They say focusing on prophecy distorts reality and diverts sincere believers from service and activity in the work of the church today.

And who can deny that there have been students of Scripture who have become so obsessed with prophecies of the future that they have neglected the present purposes of God? Their desirable quest for spiritual maturity is sidetracked for the less desirable quest of knowing more exciting speculations about future events. Balance and discernment are always needed in approaching any truth of Scripture.

Still others scoff at prophecy. They see it as mere writings of man; hard to comprehend with certainty. Yet, God seems to consider prophecy to be important: over one quarter of the canon of Scripture was prophetic prediction when it was written.

 WORD WEALTH

"The word *canon* means a "rod"—specifically, a rod with graduated marks used for measuring length. This word refers to the list of individual books that were eventually judged as authoritative and included as a part of the Old Testament and the New Testament."[1]

In both the Old and New Testaments there are whole books which are, in essence, prophecies (cf. Zech., 1 Thess., Rev.). Some have estimated that nearly ninety percent of the events prophesied in the Bible have not yet occurred!

 BEHIND THE SCENES

Dr. Wilbur M. Smith, in his book *You Can Know the Future,* has calculated there are about 165,000 "words of predictive prophecy in the Bible. This is about the equivalent of two thirds of the entire text of the New Testament. And it will come as a surprise to many, I am sure, that there is more prophetic material in Matthew, Mark, and Luke than there is prophetic material in the entire Book of Revelation."[2]

THE SPIRITUAL VALUES OF PROPHECY

In 2 Peter 1:16–19, to what does Peter compare and contrast prophecy? How does he explain its value?

How does prophecy increase our confidence in the Bible and assurance in our personal lives?

2 Tim. 3:1–5

2 Thess. 2:1–5, 15–17

How does the study of prophecy produce and encourage holy living?

Col. 3:4, 5

2 Pet. 3:1–13

How does the study of prophecy help make the unseen more real to us?

How does the study of prophecy help in times of depressing or difficult circumstances?

Rom. 5:2, 3

Rom. 8:18

2 Thess. 2:1–5

How does faith in the coming of the Lord affect our ambitions and service?

Jer. 45:5

John 5:44

How does the "blessed hope" of Christ's return affect our attitudes toward divisions within His church?

Eph. 4:1–3

Titus 2:11–13

2 Pet. 3:13–18

How does prophecy provide comfort in the face of sorrow and bereavement?

John 14:1–3

1 Thess. 4:13–18

GUIDELINES FOR INTERPRETING PROPHECY

Though biblical prophecy has been supernaturally revealed, inspired, and illuminated in our hearts by the Light of the World and by His Spirit of Truth, some passages are admittedly hard to understand. We need some guidelines for interpreting prophecy.

For instance, Daniel interpreted dreams and John of Revelation had visions. Each of these experiences is communicated with strange symbols and figures of speech. How are we to understand these? What facts of the future does God want us to understand? What does He want us to do as a result?

 BIBLE EXTRA

It is natural to study Daniel and Revelation together since something from every chapter in Daniel is either quoted or shares striking similarities in Revelation. For example, compare the following parallel passages of prophecy:

DANIEL	REVELATION
7:7	12:1–6
7:13	1:7
7:19	1:14
7:7, 20	5:5–7
7:9, 22	20:4
8:10	12:4
12:4,10	22:10–15

The **first** and most important guideline for studying prophecy is to **seek the plain and normal meaning of the words and situations described within their historical context.** Don't come to a prophetic passage with a preconceived conclusion or interpretive system to force it into. Let the grammatical and historical context communicate the plain and normal meaning, and then incorporate that meaning into what you already know.

A second guideline for interpreting prophecy is: compare one prophecy with another, especially similar prophecies. Each prophecy unfolds a bit more of the total plan of God for the ages. Often there are overlapping and corresponding references in a few or several prophecies, though they may have been delivered hundreds of years apart. (Compare the description of "the Ancient of Days" in Daniel 7:9–14 with the "One like the Son of Man" in Revelation 1:13–16 and the Lamb in chapter 5:8–14.)

A third guideline for interpreting prophecy is to **remember that the timing of the fulfillment may be uncertain.** From God's side of eternity the elements are complete and the prophecy is already fact. From man's side, separate future events may seem to blend into one, as a person looking toward a range of mountains may see two peaks as one, not perceiving the valley between them or its size and unique characteristics.

This principle suggests that biblical prophecies may have several layers of fulfillment. As examples, explain the time gap in the fulfillment of Isaiah's prophecy of Messiah's coming in the following passages:

Is. 9:6–9

Is. 11:1–5

Is. 61:1–3/Luke 4:16–21

Some of the events prophesied in the book of Daniel began to happen in the days of Babylon, Persia, and Greece during the reign of what four kings? (See Daniel 2:11—4:37; 5:1–31; 6:1–28; and 10:1—11:1.)

But those prophecies were only partially fulfilled at that time. Classical scholars would see the second-century invasion of Jerusalem by Antiochus Epiphanes (in 167–164 B.C.) as a type or partial fulfillment of yet other future events which are yet to occur at the end of this age (Dan. 9:26, 27; 11:21–35).

The fourth guideline for interpreting prophecy is sometimes called **the law of double reference.** A prophecy may have a fulfillment **both** in the time of the prophet, **and** another in the perhaps distant future. For instance, the prophetic sign given to Ahaz in Isaiah 7:14 also refers *both* to the birth of a son by Isaiah's wife (Is. 8:3) *and* to the birth of the Messiah by the Virgin Mary (Matt. 1:22; Luke 1:27).

How do the following scriptures illustrate this "law of double reference"?[3]

Deut. 28:58, 64–66

1 John 2:18

 PROBING THE DEPTHS

Even using the four guidelines for interpreting prophecy, Christians differ in their overall approach to end times prophecy. The following excerpt from the *Spirit-Filled Life Bible* lays out five common approaches. While this discussion applies most directly to how people interpret the Book of Revelation it is placed here because this guide considers Daniel and Revelation in light of each other.

• • • • • • • • •

Throughout church history, theories of interpreting end-times prophecy have been numerous and widely divergent. These have been classified as the "preterist," the "continuous historical," the "futurist," the "dispensational," and the "spiritual." Different views, however, often have been combined or intermingled, rendering all such classifications imprecise.

a. The "preterist," or "contemporary-historical," interpretation regards the visions of the book as referring primarily, if not exclusively, to events belonging to the closing decades of the first century, contemporary with the prophet John. The prophecy was concerned with the persecution of Christians instituted by the "beast," usually understood to be Nero or Domitian, and was continued by the Roman government, called "Babylon." Revelation was written to encourage believers with the hope that God would intervene, destroy the "beast," bring deliverance to His people, and establish His everlasting Kingdom. Some preterists advocate that Revelation is concerned solely with the destruction of Jerusalem, the temple, and the old era of apostate Judaism in A.D. 70.

b. According to the "continuous-historical" interpretation, Revelation contains visions that reveal in advance outstanding moments and events in human history from the days of Rome to the end of this present evil age. Within the book are discovered conjectured references to the various waves of barbarian invasions, the rise of Islam, the Protestant Reformation, the Counter-Reformation, the French Revolution, World War I, and so on. The "beast" has been identified variously as Mohammed, the Pope, Napoleon, or some subsequent dictator. The advocates of this theory ingeniously endeavor to find in European political history the fulfillment of the various visions, considered to be in chronological order.

Even though it cannot be maintained that *specific* historical events, from the second century to the present, are prophesied in Revelation, nevertheless historical events and world movements do *illustrate* repeatedly the spiritual principles set forth.

c. The "futurist" interpretation sees Revelation as primarily a prophecy concerning the denouement of history as it concerns the church in the world. The seven letters are addressed to seven historical churches; and the seals represent the forces of history—however long it may last—through which God works out His redemptive and judicial purposes leading up to the end. However, beginning with chapter 8 or 16, the events described lie entirely in the future and will attend the final disposition of God's will for human history. Revelation concludes by picturing a redeemed society dwelling in a new earth that has been purged of all evil, and with God dwelling in the midst of His people, which is the goal of the long course of redemptive history. The "futurist" interpretation is premillennial, but not dispensational. It teaches that Christ will return to establish a millennial kingdom on the Earth, but this will not be a Jewish political kingdom.

d. The "dispensational" interpretation is the most recent to appear in church history. The "dispensational" scheme of redemptive history presupposes two different peoples of God throughout history—Israel and the church—and, therefore, two programs of prophecy. The seven letters to the seven churches are interpreted "prophetically" as an outline of a seven-stage church age. Revelation 4:1 is interpreted as the Rapture of the church, understood as the secret departure of all believers to heaven before "the Great Tribulation." The rest of the book is then seen as concerned exclusively with "the Great Tribulation" and the fate of Israel at the hands of the Antichrist. According to this view, Christ returns to destroy the Beast, to bind Satan, and to introduce His thousand-year reign on Earth. Dispensationalists view this Millennium as the time when the Jewish theocracy, with the temple, the sacrificial system, and the Law of Moses, is restored and the Old Testament prophecies concerning Israel's future political triumph over the Gentiles are literally, physically fulfilled.

(Interestingly, many of Pentecostal/Charismatic tradition interpret Revelation and Daniel from this dispensational view, even though such an interpretive approach anywhere other than in prophetic scripture would dictate a denial of the present manifestation of the gifts of the Spirit.)

e. The "spiritual" or "symbolic" interpretation finds in Revelation relatively few references to *specific* events or persons of the past, present, or future, but rather the presentation of great "spiritual principles" intended to encourage and guide Christians in all geographical locations in every era of history. The successive symbolic visions set forth these principles. The living Lord Jesus Christ is victorious over the Enemy and all his allies. Those who are with Christ (the "called, chosen, and faithful," 17:14) share fully in His triumph. This reveals God as the Sovereign Ruler and Judge of the whole cosmic creation. Thus, right is ultimately vindicated in the face of wrong, justice in the face of injustice, righteousness in the face of unrighteousness. World history is moving on through tragedy and disaster to "a new heaven and a new earth."[4]

THE TIMES OF THE GENTILES

"The times of the Gentiles" is the biblical designation for a period of time between the destruction of Jerusalem in A.D. 70 (some identify it with the beginning with the Babylonian Captivity in 606 B.C.) and the Second Coming of Christ. This interval is defined by the Lord Jesus Christ as the time when Jerusalem (the city of peace) would be controlled by Gentile world powers (Luke 21:24). Many see the return of the Old City of Jerusalem to Jewish control in June of 1967 as being the end of "the times of the Gentiles" and are awaiting the imminent return of Christ.

Under divine inspiration, Daniel gives us the fullest panorama of Gentile (non-Jewish) history. Four major Gentile world empires are revealed to rule over Israel successively, only to suffer eventual doom and judgment. A comparison of Daniel 2 and 7 with Revelation 13:1–4 later in these lessons will reveal that the fourth empire, Rome, will be restored. There will be an "emperor" again (Rev. 13:3, 4), and it appears he will rule over a revived Roman Empire and provide the structure for the final fulfillment of Daniel's prophecies.

Daniel is instructed by God to "shut up the words, and seal the book, until the time of the end" (Dan. 12:4). Many feel this means that much of the detail in the book of Daniel will be obscure and irrelevant until the events of the final stage of Gentile world power remove the seal and the book of Daniel becomes fully intelligible.

EXCITING CURRENT EVENTS HELP INTERPRET PROPHECY

- The resurrection of the modern state of Israel in 1948,
- the reclamation of Jerusalem after the Six-Day War in 1967,
- the resurgence of Western Europe via the European Economic Community in the 1990's, and
- the recent 1993 Israeli-PLO peace initiatives

are just some of the exciting events which make previously obscure passages of prophecy more intelligible to today's students of Scripture. They also confirm to the discerning reader that our God is still in control of the destiny of all nations.

The lessons which follow in this *Spirit-Filled Life Bible Discovery Guide* will study in more detail the great future events in store for the Jews, the Gentiles, and the church as revealed in the great prophetic books of Daniel and Revelation and realized in the exciting events of current history. You will find these studies of mankind's future to be balanced and believable. Each one is focused on a careful exposition of Scripture and not merely the rehearsal of a human system of interpretation.

We want to gain a whole new appreciation for prophetic truth, while allowing it to do what it is ultimately designed for— to change the way we live "until the end of time."

1. "Bible—The Canon of the Bible," *Nelson's Illustrated Bible Dictionary* (Nashville, TN: Thomas Nelson Publishers, 1986), 159.

2. Wilbur M. Smith, *You Can Know the Future* (Ventura, CA: Regal Books, Gospel Light Publications, 1971), 23.

3. *Spirit-Filled Life Bible* (Nashville, TN: Thomas Nelson, Publishers, 1991), "Kingdom Dynamics: Obadiah 15, The 'Day of the Lord' in Prophecy," 1306–1307.

Lesson 2/The Issue of Integrity
Daniel 1:1–21

Daniel is not just a book of interesting visions and prophecies. It is also a study of how godly character and personal integrity can sustain us in times of stress, sickness and sensuous temptations.

Integrity may be defined as "soundness"; "adherence to a code of values"; "the quality or state of being complete or undivided." Integrity issues are complicated by the unique circumstances in which we all find ourselves from time to time. Yet they are all similar in that they are all issues of the heart. They concern our moral convictions and character.

Daniel found himself as a teenager far from home and in negative circumstances. He had been abducted from his homeland and taken to the conquering country of Babylon, where he was selected to become a trainee in the king's court. There his personal character and religious convictions were immediately tested. His personal integrity sustained him and secured a position in the king's palace and a place of prominence through the parade of two world powers and four kings.

DANIEL 1:1, 2

The Book of Daniel begins with a description of a sorrowful situation. The Holy City of Jerusalem was again surrounded by foreign troops and the surrender of all of Judah was demanded. Only this time, instead of becoming the political pawns of a powerful occupying army, the people of Judah faced a series of three mass deportations to Babylon.

In verse 1 we are introduced to two kings. Who were they and what countries did they rule?

We can learn of the background of King Jehoiakim by reading 2 Kings 23:34—24:7 and 2 Chronicles 36:1–8. Do this now in order to answer the questions below.

What was Jehoiakim's original name?

How was he made king, and by whom?

How old was Jehoiakim when he was made king of Judah, and how long did he reign?

The prophet Jeremiah was a contemporary of Jehoiakim and used by God to speak to King Jehoiakim. (See Jer. 22:18, 19; 36:27–32.) How was the king's ignominious death described?

The "therefore" in Jeremiah 22:18 refers to the previous paragraph. How did Jeremiah condemn Jehoiakim's conduct?

 AT A GLANCE

In Jehoiakim's third year of reign (Daniel 1:1) as a vassal king under the hand of Pharaoh Necho of Egypt, Judah found itself in the middle of a war between the two super-powers of that day: Egypt and Babylon. In 605 B.C., the army of Nebuchadnezzar II of Babylon and the army of Pharaoh Necho of Egypt collided at Carchemish, the ancient Mesopotamian capital of the Hittites. The Egyptian army suffered a decisive defeat, allowing the Babylonians to assume control of the Syro-Palestinian region, ending nearly 300 years of Assyrian supremacy (885–607 B.C.). Many historians view this defeat of the Egyptians at Carchemish as one of the most important battles of the ancient world.

Nebuchadnezzar's Campaigns Against Judah (605–586 B.C.). From 605 B.C. to 586 B.C. Judah suffered repeated Babylonian invasions. The final blow came from the southern approach to Jerusalem.[2]

    BIBLE EXTRA

As Pharaoh Necho made his march northward to encounter Nebuchadnezzar's army, Jehoiakim's father, King Josiah, tried to block his advance but was fatally wounded in the battle. (Read 2 Chron. 35:20–25.)

How old was Josiah when he was made King of Judah? How long did he reign? How old was he when he died in battle against Pharaoh Necho? (See 2 Chron. 34:1.)

After the Battle of Carchemish in 605 B.C., Nebuchadnezzar pursued Pharoah Necho and his army as they retreated back toward Egypt over the land-bridge of Palestine. When Nebuchadnezzar saw the beautiful city of Jerusalem sitting on the Judean hills, he surrounded it and demanded its surrender. Some historians speculate that Nebuchadnezzar not only was impressed with the beautiful city and its fortifications, but remembered having heard stories of its wealth.

While at Jerusalem, Nebuchadnezzar received word that his father, Nabopolassar, had died. Consequently, he had to hurry home to Babylon to prevent any moves against his Neo-Babylonian/Chaldean dynasty.

Since he had not finished setting up his administration in Jerusalem, he needed a puppet king. Nebuchadnezzar admired Jehoiakim for his loyalty to the Pharoah of Egypt, so he decided to leave him as a willing vassal on the throne of Judah. But before leaving, Nebuchadnezzar took all of the vessels of value from "the house of God" in Jerusalem back to the house of his god in "the land of Shinar," which is another name for Babylon, modern southeastern Iraq.

Why would Nebuchadnezzar rob the temple?

What implications could this have about the relative powers of the God of the Jews and the god of Nebuchadnezzar?

When had something like this happened in Jewish history before? (See 1 Sam. 5:1, 2.)

DANIEL 1:3–16

Nebuchadnezzar, however, also wisely took measures to guarantee Jehoiakim's loyalty and to make sure that during his absence the Jews would not revolt against his Chaldean Empire. (See vv. 3, 4.)

Who was Ashpenaz? What was he instructed to do?

History indicates that fifty to seventy young men were taken as hostages from the royal family or other families of nobility in Judah in the first deportation of 605 B.C. Ashpenaz was responsible for the selection and training of the young men ("children of Israel") to learn the Chaldean language and culture.

Why do you suppose the Babylonians selected young men for such training?

What did the king assign to the young men? (v. 5)

How would teenage boys you know respond to this royal treatment?

How long was the training period to last?

A part of the Jewish training would be a thorough exposure to the dietary section of the Mosaic Law. Not only would Daniel have learned to recite these laws, but his parents would have practiced them in their home, as well (Lev. 10:11; Deut. 6:7–9).

FAITH ALIVE

Though Daniel's parents, priests, and prophets were not available for guidance, he knew that the royal food and wine would not be prepared in accordance with the Jewish dietary laws. But, perhaps more importantly, there was the real possibility that they would have been served meat and wine that had been offered to idols, as was the custom in pagan cultures (Deut. 32:38; 1 Cor. 10:18–21). To eat of that food they would have been participating in a pagan feast.

Where are we to draw the line in questionable, culturally accepted activities? (See 1 Thess. 4:1–12 and Col. 3:1–11.)

In Colossians 3:12–17 the Apostle Paul offers a strategy to help us live for God day by day. In your own words, list the six principles presented by Paul.

1.

2.

3.

4.

5.

6.

Whether in the area of music, dress, or social codes and activities, few modern teenagers will take a sanctified stand against the socially "in" thing. However, Daniel's religious roots and spiritual heritage helped him resolve in his heart not to compromise and defile himself with even royal "delicacies."

As far as we know, only Daniel, Shadrach, Meshach, and Abed-Nego took a stand to separate themselves toward the Lord, and away from the things which would defile them. The rest of the hostages became "good Chaldeans" and went into obscurity. But the integrity and character qualities of these three teenagers are read and studied to this day!

Daniel knew he was right and he pursued his request to the palace officer who was responsible for their daily provisions.

He proposed a ten-day test. What was it? (See Dan. 1:12, 13.)

What was the result of the test? (See Dan. 1:15, 16.)

At the end of the testing period the four Hebrew lads looked healthier and trimmer than all the other trainees. By resisting the pressures of the culture and pursuing a godly commitment, they were not only pleasing God, they were eating things that were healthful, and it even showed in their faces.

DANIEL 1:17–20

How did the four Hebrews learn the literature and wisdom of that day?

When is education an enemy of God?

Does God need wise and competent leaders in our culture?

According to Daniel 1:17–20, what did Daniel have that the others did not?

In what ways were the four Hebrews like and unlike the occult "magicians and astrologers" who were advisors to King Nebuchadnezzar?

DANIEL 1:21

Daniel's life and ministry encompassed the entire Babylonian period and reached into the Persian phase of world history. He arrived in Babylon in the first deportation from Jerusalem in 605 B.C. and lived to see the first exiles return to Jerusalem to restore the temple in 538 B.C.

We are not told what influence Daniel may have had in this important fulfillment of scripture at the hand of Cyrus the Great, but lessons on the sovereignty of God are to be learned throughout Daniel. God will ultimately judge Gentile nations. And God will ultimately rescue, resurrect, and reward Israel, God's chosen nation.

1. *Merriam-Webster's Collegiate Dictionary*, 10th ed. (Springfield, MA: 1993), 608.
2. *Spirit-Filled Life Bible* (Nashville, TN: Thomas Nelson Publishers, 1991), 567.

Lesson 3/Disturbing Dreams and Details
Daniel 2:1—6:28

Dreams always had a prominent place in the lives of ancient peoples. They were considered to convey messages from God, and were frequently thought to be predictive in nature. Because of that, the images, thoughts, and impressions conveyed during dreams were always interpreted and pondered—especially when experienced by religious and political leaders.

Among the ancient Babylonians, Daniel became known as an interpreter of dreams. He and the other Hebrew "children" were known to be among the wisest of the king's advisors, but Daniel's gift of "understanding in all visions and dreams" (Dan. 1:17, 20) made him especially important during the reigns of Nebuchadnezzar, Belshazzar, and Darius (Daniel 2—6). His apocalyptic visions (Daniel 3—8) give a glimpse of mankind's future, even until the end of time.

BEHIND THE SCENES

The Book of Daniel is written in two languages: from 2:4 to the end of chapter 7 the language is Aramaic; elsewhere it is Hebrew. Some have suggested that Aramaic was the Gentile language of commerce and diplomacy over the whole known world. Therefore the section which gives the general outline of the whole course of "the times of the Gentiles" would be in Aramaic, and the later visions, which related especially to the people of the Covenant would be written in Hebrew.

THE FORGOTTEN DREAM
DANIEL 2:1–16

In the second year of Nebuchadnezzar's reign he had a disturbing dream which he could not remember the next morning. Apparently he had been in bed, reflecting on the cataclysmic changes which had happened in world events to move the balance of military might from the Assyrians and Egyptians to his own kingdom of Babylon. Nebuchadnezzar wondered, "What will come to pass after this," or "What will happen in human history after my kingdom comes to an end?" As he went to sleep, God revealed the answer in a symbolic dream which was so shocking he was unable to sleep (v. 1), but also unable to remember the details!

It was this forgotten dream which made him demand of the brain trust of Babylon, "the magicians, the astrologers, the sorcerers and the Chaldeans," to tell him the dream and to interpret its meaning.

What did he threaten to do to them and their homes?

How was this similar to what happened in 2 Kings 10:27?

What was their response to the king? (Dan. 2:7, 10).

What was his reaction?

What did they say was the only source from which such information could be available?

Filled with anger, the king made a rash and radical command. What was it and how did it affect Daniel and his three Hebrew friends?

What was Daniel's response?

 BEHIND THE SCENES

Nebuchadnezzar summoned a select group who served as counselors to the king's court. The first three groups mentioned are your typical tabloid-trio:

- The **magicians** were occultic fortune-tellers.
- The **astrologers** charted the positions of the stars and claimed to determine destinies on the basis of how they were arranged, much like the authors of horoscopes claim to do today.
- The **sorcerers** were mediums who attempted to talk with the dead via demons.

The **Chaldeans** were mentioned last, but may have been the leading group among the "king's cabinet" because they seem to do the talking in this passage. Several ancient authors use this term to denote priests and other persons educated in the classical arts and sciences of Chaldea (Babylon), especially in traditions of astronomy and astrology.

"Some scholars believe the 'wise men [magi] from the East' (Matt. 2:1) who came to Jerusalem at the time of Jesus' birth may have been Chaldean astrologers."[1]

THE DREAM OF DESTINY
DANIEL 2:17–45

What follows is the most comprehensive revelation of Gentile world history found anywhere in the Bible. It is a prophetic panorama which stretches from more than 600 years before Christ's first coming, to His millennial reign after His Second

Coming. This "dream of destiny" affirms that God is in control of world affairs, and human history is really "His story."

How did God reveal Nebuchadnezzar's dream to Daniel? (Dan. 2:19)

What was Daniel's response to God? (vv. 20–23)

Showing courtesy and winsome humility to the king, Daniel disclaimed all personal ability in succeeding where the wise men in Babylon had failed. However, Daniel did exalt his God, Jehovah, by saying: "There is a God in heaven who reveals secrets, and he has made known to King Nebuchadnezzar what will be in the latter days" (v. 28). This phrase, "in the latter days," refers to the future—from that time forward through all of human history.

The giant statue in Nebuchadnezzar's dream represented the four kingdoms that would dominate as world powers. Carefully read the account of the dream (2:24–45), and identify the material which related to the following part(s) of the statue:

Part	Material
Head	_____
Chest and Arms	_____
Belly and Thighs	_____
Legs and Feet	_____

BEHIND THE SCENES

Daniel's interpretation of the image (Dan. 2:36–43), needs to be studied in concert with his vision of the four beasts in Daniel 7 (vv. 1–7, 17) and the facts of history. Accordingly, many dispensational scholars readily recognize the implied empires as the Babylonian Empire (605–539 B.C.), the Medo-Persian Empire (539–331 B.C.), the Grecian Empire (331–168 B.C.), and the Roman Empire (168 B.C. to approximately 476 B.C.), symbolized, after its division, by the two legs of iron. These four successive kingdoms each developed in history, prospered, and disappeared in the order a Daniel predicted. (See Daniel 2:38; 5:28,31; 8:20, 21.)

It was under a decree by the fourth Gentile power, Rome, that Jesus' birth occurred in Bethlehem (Luke 2:1). Paul explained that this appointed time for the coming of Christ was in "the fullness of time" (Gal. 4:4, 5), when world conditions favored His appearance and the propagation of His gospel.

Rome, rather than succumbing to a succeeding empire, broke into a number of smaller kingdoms in the fourth and fifth centuries A.D. Later, they became the nations of Europe.

Who or what does the "stone" symbolize? (See Gen. 49:24, Is. 28:16; Matt. 21:42–44; Acts 4:10–12, 1 Pet. 2:4–8.)

Compare Daniel 2:44 with 7:27, 1 Corinthians 15:24, and Revelation 11:15. What do these verses indicate that God wants us to comprehend most about His kingdom?

DANIEL IS PRAISED AND PROMOTED
DANIEL 2:46–49

What does Nebuchadnezzar do in the emotion of the moment? (v. 46)

Why did the king acknowledge the true and living God? (v. 47)

What did the king do to promote Daniel?

How did Daniel use his new position to help his three Hebrew friends?

THE PROVIDENCE OF GOD AND THE LAST DAYS
DANIEL 2—6

God's providence during the Jewish Exile is seen in the details of several events which occurred during the successive reigns of three kings: Nebuchadnezzar, Belshazzar, and Darius. It is shown

- in Daniel's rise to prominence in Nebuchadnezzar's court (ch. 2);
- in the dramatic intervention of one "like the Son of god" in the fiery-furnace trial (ch. 3);
- in Nebuchadnezzar's temporary insanity (ch. 4);
- in the divine graffiti predicting Babylon's fall during Belshazzar's banquet (ch. 5); and
- in the miraculous deliverance of Daniel from the ravenous lions during the reign of Darius the Mede (ch. 6).

THE IMAGE OF GOLD
DANIEL 3:1–7

Nebuchadnezzar's power and position allowed him to become filled with pride. Obsessed with himself and his supposed accomplishments, he determined to exalt himself in the eyes of the people by building a skyscraper-size statue of himself —a symbol of his power and the perpetuity of his kingdom.

A cubit is about eighteen inches. Convert the image's dimensions to feet. (See Dan. 3:1.)

What material was the image made of? Do you think it was solid or just covered with this material?

Do you think there is any relation to this chosen material and Daniel's interpretation of Nebuchadnezzar's dream? (Dan. 2:37, 38)

When the royal band played at the elaborate dedication ceremonies for the king's statue, what were the "peoples, nations, and languages" to do? (Dan. 3:4–6)

Some believe King Nebuchadnezzar was trying to unite all the religions of his world empire by building the enormous image and requiring everyone to bow before it. What was to be the penalty for nonconformity? (Dan. 3:6)

THE CHARGE OF TREASON
DANIEL 3:8–18

Who were the "nonconformists" in Nebuchadnezzar's kingdom and what were their official positions? (Dan. 3:12)

THE TEST OF FIRE
DANIEL 3:19–30

How did the king respond to the remarks of commitment to God by the Hebrew young men? (vv. 19–23)

As Nebuchadnezzar stood watching the execution of his orders, he was astonished at the preservation of these Hebrews. What did he and the other officials see? What observations did they make about them? (vv. 24–27)

 FAITH ALIVE

The courageous and uncompromising stand of Shadrach, Meshach, and Abed-Nego has been and continues to be an inspiration to the people of God when tempted to waver in our walk of faith.

What can we learn from this fiery furnace about future persecution and preservation for God's people?

What promise can we claim from such scriptures as 1 Corinthians 10:13 and Isaiah 43:1–3?

NEBUCHADNEZZAR'S SECOND DREAM
DANIEL 4:1–27

This chapter is unique in that it appears to be a state paper in which King Nebuchadnezzar gives his own personal testimony of "the signs and wonders that the Most High God has worked for me" (Dan. 4:2). The preamble to the proclamation (Dan. 4:1–3) continues to magnify God, whose "kingdom is an everlasting kingdom, and [whose] dominion is from generation to generation."

Nebuchadnezzar's narration continues with a recounting of his temporary insanity and loss of control of his kingdom for seven years. But his time of "flourishing in his palace" (Dan. 4:4) is once again disturbed by a dream. Again Daniel is called upon to interpret the dream, since the court counselors cannot.

Why do you suppose God repeatedly spoke to Nebuchadnezzar in dreams and visions? (See Job 33:14–17.)

How was this disturbing dream-vision different than the first? (Compare Dan. 2:3–11 with 4:4–18.)

In Daniel 4:19, Daniel reluctantly begins to relate the interpretation of the dream. To whom did he say he wished it applied?

What advice did Daniel give the king at the close of the interpretation of the dream? (v. 27)

NEBUCHADNEZZAR'S HUMILIATION
DANIEL 4:28–33

Twelve months later the judgment expressed by the dream fell upon Nebuchadnezzar. He became beastly insane, and was driven from men, and lost his kingdom. A terrible humiliation for the proud, boastful king of a world empire (Dan. 4:1)!

  BIBLE EXTRA

"The tree which the king saw in the dream represented himself. The order to fell the great tree was prophetic of a temporary form of insanity known as lycanthropy in which a man imagines himself to be some form of animal. The word derives from Greek *lukos,* or 'wolf,' and *anthropos,* meaning 'man.'

"During this diseased period, Nebuchadnezzar would find it impossible to continue with the affairs of state (Dan. 4:25). Yet control would not be irretrievable, since the stump with its root would be left (Dan. 4:26).

"The purpose of the lycanthropy was to remind the king of the transcendent sovereignty of the Lord (Dan. 4:25). The same assertion was made one year later when the sentence was executed (Dan. 4:32).

"Nebuchadnezzar's lycanthropy was not a light case. The king was so thoroughly deluded by hallucinations of his new role as beast that he was driven from the palace and from polite society."[2]

NEBUCHADNEZZAR PRAISES GOD
DANIEL 4:34–37

After "seven times" (which could mean seven months, seasons, or years) of this humiliating experience had passed over him, Nebuchadnezzar was suddenly restored to sanity and began blessing the God of heaven for His mercy (Dan. 4:34).

What did Nebuchadnezzar suggest was the cause of downfalls? (Dan. 4:37)

Compare Nebuchadnezzar's assessment with that of Solomon in Proverbs 16:18.

BELSHAZZAR'S FEAST
DANIEL 5:1–12

The year was 539 B.C. Nearly seventy years had passed since Daniel was brought to Babylon, and Belshazzar, the grandson of Nebuchadnezzar, now ruled from the thrown there. Historical inscriptions show that he was co-regent with his father,

Nabonidus, who maintained a separate royal residence at Tema, Arabia. Jeremiah settles any confusion by saying that "all nations shall serve him [Nebuchadnezzar], and his son and his son's son, until the very time of his land comes" (Jer. 27:7).

As this chapter begins, Nabonidus and his forces had been defeated and he was exiled by Cyrus, the king of the Medes and Persians. The conquering Medo-Persians then turned their attention to Belshazzar, the de facto king, and besieged the city of Babylon.

In a show of confidence and implied indifference to the military threat outside the well-fortified walls of the city of Babylon, Belshazzar ordered a momentous celebration, which quickly degenerated into a drunken orgy. Belshazzar, himself setting the bad example before his guests, wives, and concubines (Dan. 1:1), ordered the gold and silver vessels, which Nebuchadnezzar had taken from the temple of Jehovah in Jerusalem, to be brought in for drinking wine and the praising of pagan deities (Dan. 1:3, 4). This blasphemous use of the sacred vessels was perhaps to demonstrate the superiority of the Babylonian deities over the God of the Hebrews.

At the height of the revelry in the riotous feast, God wrote a mysterious message on the plastered wall with human fingers, eerily disconnected from any hand!

How did this action affect Belshazzar? (See Dan. 1:6.)

To whom did the king turn for help in interpreting the writing?

What did he offer them as a reward? Did it help?

Of what did the queen (or queen mother) remind the king?

THE MYSTERIOUS WRITING IS EXPLAINED
DANIEL 5:13–29

The old prophet Daniel was ushered before the king. The same offers and bribes were made to him as had been made to the king's wise men to make known the interpretation of the mysterious writing.

What was offered, and how did Daniel respond?

What do you think you would have done if you were in Daniel's place that night?

Daniel gave Belshazzar a history lesson from his own family tree. He reminded him of the humiliating experiences of his grandfather, Nebuchadnezzar, whose sanity was removed and who was driven from his throne for "seven times." Then the prophet indicted Belshazzar on three charges. Read Daniel 5:22, 23 and state the charges.

First:

Second:

Third:

When transliterated into English the mysterious words were: *Mene, Mene, Tekel, Upharsin.* With God's help, Daniel gave the meaning of each word. Basically the interpretation related to Belshazzar's kingdom, himself, and the future of Babylon. Write the specific interpretation for each word.

MENE:

TEKEL:

PERES (the verb form of UPHARSIN):

Compare Daniel 4:37 with 5:22 to find a common reason for the decline and demise of leaders and nations.

BELSHAZZAR AND BABYLON FALL IN A NIGHT
DANIEL 5:30

That very night Belshazzar, the king of Babylon, was slain (Dan. 5:30). The greatest empire humanity had ever known was about to fall without a battle. With King Nabonidus exiled and the Babylonian leaders drunk, the city of Babylon was taken that night by Cyrus, who secretly diverted the Euphrates River and sent his Persian troops under the city walls on the river bed. They easily overpowered the Babylonians, who were in drunken disarray within. Babylon, the head of gold in Nebuchadnezzar's dream, was no more.

According to Acts 17:26 how are the times and boundaries of nations pre-appointed and controlled?

Can this appointment be changed or controlled by man? (See Dan. 4:35.)

Why should we pray for national and local leaders? (See 1 Tim. 2:1–4.)

THE PLOT AGAINST DANIEL
DANIEL 6:1–9

Upon the death of Belshazzar and the fall of Babylon, Darius the Mede ascended the throne. Opinions differ as to the exact identification of Darius. Some indicate that the word *Darius* is not a name, but a Median title, meaning "His Majesty" or "the Royal One," and that the man who assumed the title was Gubaru, who was one of the commanders of the armies of the Medes. Meanwhile, Cyrus, as the commander of the Persians, was engaged in military affairs that occupied him for most of his reign. Others believe *Darius* is a title of honor or significance, and was used by Cyrus himself.

What administrative structure did Darius set up over the kingdom?

What gave Daniel an edge in distinguishing himself above the other governmental leaders?

 BIBLE EXTRA

When a conqueror seeks to set up a new government over a subjugated nation, he is faced with a difficult and dangerous situation. It is easier and more effective to win the cooperation of the people than to force their allegiance. Darius was shrewd enough to see that by making Daniel Prime Minister he would not only continue a popular rule, but he would have in Daniel a trusted statesman who had long been familiar with the conditions in Babylon and had ruled with loyalty and success. Daniel's career and his character were spotless.

What was behind the plot to depose Daniel? (6:1–9)

How did the proposal presented to the king appeal to him?

DANIEL IN THE LIONS' DEN
DANIEL 6:10–23

Though Daniel was carefully excluded from the earlier discussions, he was nonetheless aware that Darius had signed the decree prohibiting prayer to God. Undaunted, Daniel went back to his rooftop prayer chamber and continued his daily discipline, praying to God "evening and morning and at noon . . ." (Ps. 55:17).

What other options might have been open to Daniel?

 FAITH ALIVE

The early disciples were commanded by Jewish leaders not to teach in the name of Jesus (Acts 5:28). Peter's response presented a principle for any time the laws of men conflict with the laws of God. In such times, "we ought to obey God rather than men" (v. 29).

Can you think of any issues today which pit the law of the land against the law of God?

If so, what can be learned from Daniel's example in chapter 6?

What further information is learned about the decree Darius signed? (6:10–15)

How did the conspirators describe Daniel's disregard for the decree? (v. 13)

How did Darius react to their information? (v. 14)

The other leaders pressed the king to fulfill his oath, and he saw that he had no choice but to deliver Daniel to the lions' den. Yet the king was quick to communicate confidence that Daniel's God would deliver him.

The king had an anxious night, and at dawn he ran quickly to the den of lions. With a grieved spirit Darius cried out to Daniel to inquire if his God had indeed been able to deliver him.

Where would Daniel have been if God had not delivered him that night? (See 2 Cor. 5:6–8.)

Who did Daniel say had "shut the lions' mouths"?

How was Daniel delivered? (v. 23)

DARIUS HONORS DANIEL AND HIS GOD
DANIEL 6:24–28

What was the horrible fate of Daniel's enemies and their families? (v. 24)

How did the pagan king honor the God of Daniel? (vv. 25–27)

How do you explain the destruction of Daniel's enemies and the fact that Daniel "prospered in the reign of Darius, and [even] in the reign of Cyrus the Persian"? (Dan. 6:28)

 FAITH ALIVE

What kind of "lions" are you facing?

Describe a time you were unjustly accused or unfairly convicted in a matter?

Are you willing to surrender to God's will regardless of what happens in your "den of lions"?

Based on the stories of the young men in the fire (Dan. 3) and of Daniel's deliverance from the lions, write your own affirmation of faith regarding the difficult circumstance you have described above.

1. "Chaldeans," *Nelson's Illustrated Bible Dictionary* (Nashville, TN: Thomes Nelson Publishers, 1986), 215.

2. *The Believer's Study Bible* (Nashville, TN: Thomas Nelson Publishers, 1991), 1186–1187, notes on Daniel 4:19, 32, 33.

3. Ibid., 1188, note on Daniel 5:1.

Lesson 4/A Panorama of Prophecy
Daniel 7:1—8:27

Someone has said, "Prophecy is history written down before it happens!"

One of the exciting elements of biblical prophecy is that it accurately predicts aspects of the future. God alone is omniscient and knows the future, but He has willed to reveal through His prophets His unchangeable redemptive plan for human history during "the times of the Gentiles."

Because the prophet Daniel "had understanding in all visions and dreams" (Dan. 1:17), he could interpret other people's dreams and visions. But he was also specially used by God to receive and relate four key visions about future events which form a kind of panorama of prophecy. These are recounted through a series of signs and symbols in the final chapters of his writings.

In Daniel 7, the prophet describes the four nations he saw earlier in Nebuchadnezzar's statue-dream as beasts emerging from the sea. The description and perspective are different, but the same nations are in view. Nebuchadnezzar's dream detailed Gentile world history from man's perspective, while Daniel perceived these "times of the Gentiles" from God's vantage point.

Like the four metals of the image in Daniel 2, the four beasts of chapter 7 represent four world empires. In a related vision, Daniel foretells forthcoming events and the climaxing conflict of the world's superpowers (ch. 8). Thus, the prophecies of Daniel 2, 7, and 8 parallel each other in their universal scope and specific sequence.

AT A GLANCE

World Empire	Nebuchadnezzar's Dream Monument	Daniel's First Vision	Daniel's Second Vision
Babylon (606–538 B.C.)	Head of Gold (2:32, 37, 38)	Lion (7:4)	
Medo-Persia (538–331 B.C.)	Breast, arms of silver (2:32, 39)	Bear (7:5)	Ram (8:3, 4, 20)
Greece (331–146 B.C.)	Belly, thighs of brass (2:32, 39)	Leopard (7:6)	Goat with one horn (8:5–8, 21) Four horns (8:8, 22) Little horn (8:9–14)
Rome (146 B.C.–A.D. 476)	Legs of iron Feet of iron and clay (2:33, 40, 41)	Strong beast (7:7, 11, 19, 23)	

FAITH ALIVE

How was Daniel affected emotionally and physically by his visions? (See Dan. 7:15, 28; 8:17, 18, 27; 10:8.)

Some people seem to get "religious pride" when they grasp a certain knowledge of Bible prophecy. How should we respond when we understand God's prophetic Word?

List the practical instruction Jesus delivers with prophetic prediction in these verses:

Matt. 24:42–44; 25:13

Matt. 25:1–13,

BIBLE EXTRA

A comparison of Daniel 2 and Daniel 7 with Revelation 13:1–4 indicates to dispensationalists that the fourth empire, Rome, was never totally destroyed. Only the imperial *form* of its social and political powers came to an end. Many feel that near the conclusion of "the latter days" imperial Rome will be restored in some fashion and be ruled by "the beast," the apocalyptic Antichrist who will be empowered by Satan himself.

VISION OF THE FOUR BEASTS
DANIEL 7:1–8

In Daniel 7—12, Daniel relates four key visions about future events. These do not necessarily fit in chronological order with the events of the preceding chapters. For instance, in chapter 7, "Daniel's dream would have been about 550 B.C. This would have been some 10 years before the events of chapter 5."[1]

In Daniel 7 we actually have four visions. The first one is seen in vv. 2–6. The scene is one of a great storm breaking forth on the "Great Sea," resulting in the emergence of a great beast from the sea after each storm.

THE FOUR WINDS AND
THE FOUR BEASTS FROM THE GREAT SEA
DANIEL 7:2–8

Daniel's vision shows human history in turmoil. "Four" is a number that is often used in reference to the things of this earth: "four seasons," "four corners," etc. "Winds" in symbolic passages refer to wars, strife, demonic activity, and judgments from God (vv. 1–3; 8:7–13 with Jer. 25:32, 33; Rev. 7:1–3). Finally, "beasts" are often seen in symbolic passages representing kingdoms (Dan. 7:17; 23, 24; 8:20–23; Rev. 17:8–11) and their rulers (Rev. 11:7; 13:18; 17:8). Each beast, emerging from the sea, typifies a great world empire coming forth to run its course.

Match the details from Daniel's visions of the wild animals (7:4–8) with the proper beast: the lion, the bear, the leopard, and the "dreadful beast."

Vision Detail	Corresponding Beast
Human eyes	
Four heads	
Eagle's wings	
Mouth speaking pompous words	
Man's heart given to it	
Iron teeth	
Three ribs in its mouth	
Ten horns	
Little horn	
Four wings of a bird on its back	

THE VISION OF THE FIFTH KINGDOM: THE KINGDOM OF GOD DANIEL 7:9–14

The context links the four Gentile world powers with a literal, earthly kingdom of God, which follows them.

What titles does Daniel use to introduce the concept of the Trinity? Dan. 7:9, 13, and 22

The first term portrays God on His throne, judging the great world empires of Daniel's day. The second is thought to be the Lord Jesus coming in the clouds of heaven (v. 13) to claim his rightful earthly inheritance from His Father, the Ancient of Days.

How was this predicted by the following?

David (Ps. 2:6–9):

Gabriel (Luke 1:32):

Jesus (Mark 14:61, 62):

  BIBLE EXTRA

Whenever Jesus referred to himself as "the Son of man," he was purposely lining Himself up with Daniel's prophecy of the coming Messiah (Matt. 16:27, 28; 19:28; 25:31; 26:64). Compare Daniel's vision of the coronation of Christ with its counterpart in Revelation 4 and 5:

Daniel 7:13, 14	Rev. 4:2b–4; 10b, 14	Rev. 5:1a, 4, 5, 7, 12, 13

DANIEL'S VISION IS INTERPRETED
DANIEL 7:15–28

Who is to possess the kingdom and for what duration? (Dan. 7:18, 27)

Identify the various "saints" (or "holy ones") of the ages in the following verses and indicate if you think they will be included in "the kingdom, forever, even forever and ever":

Ps. 34:9a

Ps. 116:15

Ps. 149:1

1 Cor. 1:2a

Rev. 20:4

The "little horn" is said to persecute (literally "wear out") the saints of the Most High. This seems to suggest mental affliction and circumstantial aggravation more than bodily harm. How does this compare with the sufferings during the Great Tribulation? (See Rev. 7:4–17; 12:13–17.)

How may we apply Daniel 7:21 and 22 to our own spiritual warfare?

What does this passage of scripture reveal about Satan's strategy towards all believers?

How can it prepare us for spiritual adversity?

Who else are specifically promised a place in the kingdom? On what basis? (See Matt. 19:28, Rom. 4:3, 21–25; 2 Cor. 5:21.)

Who helped interpret the meaning of the four beasts to Daniel? (See Dan. 7:16, and compare with Dan. 8:16; 9:21.)

What do the ten horns (Dan. 7:7, 8, 23, 24) symbolize? Compare these horns with those mentioned in Revelation 13 and 17.

When will the "little horn" (Dan. 7:8) arise on the political scene? (See 7:24, 25; Rev. 17:8–11.)

How long will he manifest intense persecution of "the saints of the Most High," and seek to change times and law (Dan. 7:25)? Compare the length of his brief career with Rev. 11:2, 3; 12:6, 14; 13:5.

What will cause his career to come to a sudden and disastrous end? (Dan. 7:26, 27)

PROBING THE DEPTHS

"The prophecy [of Dan 7:21, 22] unveils the present age of the kingdom, which is one of ongoing struggle—with victory upon victory for the church. Yet it withholds its conclusive triumph until Christ comes again.

"This prophecy also balances the question of divine sovereignty and human responsibility: (1) God's sovereignty accomplishes the foundational victory (v. 22) and in the Cross achieves the decisive victory allowing the saints new dimensions for advance and conquest; (2) He entrusts the responsibility for that advance to His own to "possess the kingdom," entering into conflict with the adversary, at times at the expense of their apparent defeat (v. 26). (3) However, movement toward victory is theirs as they press the 'judgment' of the 'court' (vv. 22, 26) and seize realms controlled by evil. They wrestle the dominion from hellish powers, continuing in warfare until the ultimate seating of the Son of Man (vv. 24, 27).

"Prophetic systems vary as to how and when these words unfold on the calendar of church history, for the passage is subject to different schemes of interpretation, each with different projected chronologies. But the foundational fact remains that an agelong struggle between 'the saints' and the power of evil in the world calls each believer to a commitment to steadfast battle, a mixture of victories with setbacks, and a consummate triumph anticipated at Christ's Coming. In the meantime, we 'receive' the kingdom and pursue victories for our King, by His power, making intermittent gains—all of which are based on 'the judgment' achieved through the Cross. (See 1 Pet. 2:9 and Rev. 12:10, 11.)"[3]

THE VISION OF A WARRING RAM AND GOAT
DANIEL 8:1–14

Two years after Daniel's visions of the four beasts, he saw another vision which gave additional information on some key questions. The time of this vision was at the end of Belshazzar's reign (approximately 547 B.C.) and corresponds to the dramatic events of the fifth chapter of Daniel.

The earlier, historical section, Daniel 2:4 through 7:28, was written in Aramaic, the commercial language of the Gentile world of that day. Perhaps the prophet used Aramaic here to emphasize the destinies of the Gentile nations: their rise, progress, decline, and collapse. Daniel 8—12, however, emphasizes the destiny of the Hebrew people. These chapters focus on human history as it relates to the Jews; and the original language of the text is appropriately Hebrew.

In the vision of Daniel 8:1–14, Daniel is taken to the palace at Shushan (or Susa), the winter capital of the Persian kings, about 230 miles east of Babylon. The "River Ulai" (v. 2) was actually an irrigation canal that flowed northwest to the city between the Kerkha and the Abdizful Rivers. There he sees a battle between a two-horned ram and a one-horned goat.

Describe the unique features of the ram of verses 4 and 5.

From which direction did the goat come, and what happened when he confronted the ram?

What happened after the powerful horn of the goat was broken? (v. 8)

 BEHIND THE SCENES

"The breaking of the notable horn [v. 8] was a reference to the untimely death of Alexander in 323 B.C. at the apex of his strength. His kingdom was divided among his four generals (called the *diadochi,* Gk., **'successors'**) Ptolemy, Cassander, Lysimachus, and Seleucus 1, the four horns which arose in place of Alexander. Lysimachus received Thrace and Bithynia, Cassander took Macedonia and Greece, Seleucus 1 received Syria, Babylonia, and the East as far as India, while Ptolemy staked out Egypt, Palestine, and Arabia."[4]

Out of Syria came Antiochus IV, surnamed Epiphanes (Gr. "God manifest"). He ruled Syria from 175 B.C. to 163 B.C. and persecuted the Jews and profaned their temple, becoming known as the Old Testament Antichrist.

"In bitter reprisal against the Jews, Antiochus attacked Jerusalem, killing 50,000 men, women, and children. He sold an additional 40,000 people into slavery. The temple was dedicated to Jupiter Olympus; and on the great bronze altar a sow was offered, the juices of which were liberally spread throughout the temple precincts. He used harlots in the temple to celebrate Saturnalia and forbade the observance of the Sabbath, the reading of Scripture, and circumcision. Verses 10–12 apparently refer to all of this. Small wonder that Antiochus was also called Epimanes, i.e., 'Antiochus the madman.' "[5]

"Classical interpretation identifies this 'little horn' with the one mentioned in Daniel 7:8, while dispensational interpretation does not."[6]

Historians identify Antiochus Epiphanes' stopping of sacrifices in the Jewish temple in Jerusalem as beginning in September, 171 B.C. On December 15, 168 B.C. he desecrated the temple by sacrificing the sow in what the Jews termed "the abomination of desolation." The Jewish revolt which followed, led by Judas Maccabaeus ("the hammer"), is described in two Apocryphal books, 1 and 2 Maccabees.

Finally, in December, 165 B.C., the Jewish patriots cleansed and rededicated the temple Antiochus had defiled. It is interesting to note that working backwards 2300 days (Dan. 8:14), one arrives at the season in 171 B.C. when Antiochus began his harassment of the Jews.

The celebration of this cleansing of the temple later became a Jewish holiday known as the Feast of Dedication (John 10:22). Today it is known as Hanukkah and the Feast of Lights.

Some religious interpreters have made the 2300 days (literally "evening-mornings," perhaps referring to the evening and morning sacrifices) stand for years and have tried to arrive at the year of Christ's return. In each instance they have been embarrassed by their inaccurate predictions.

According to Daniel 8:14, 15, how long will the "little horn" do away with the daily sacrifices in the Jewish temple at Jerusalem?

Convert the answer into a period of so many years, months, and days.

Compare this period with the one mentioned in Revelation 12:14. What is significant in this comparison?

THE VISION IS INTERPRETED
DANIEL 8:15–24

The vision of the ram and goat symbolizes what period of time? (Dan. 8:17, 19)

The two-horned ram represents which kings? (v. 20)

The male goat represents which world power? (v. 21)

When will the "little horn" (vv. 9–12) come to power? (vv. 22, 23)

Antiochus Epiphanes may have been a historical "little horn," but there is yet a prophetical "little horn" (the Antichrist) who will do all his forerunner did and much more. See Revelation 12, 13, and 19, and list similarities with the "little horn" of Daniel 8:9–20, 23–27.

Compare the instruction given to Daniel in 8:26 with that of 12:4.

The shutting and sealing of a vision was a common feature of apocalyptic literature (Is. 8:16). Its meaning is clarified in Revelation.

Why do you think Daniel fainted and was sick after hearing the interpretation to the vision? Check Dan. 9:3, 10:2 and 3 before answering.

All biblical truth, including prophecy, is intended to make the believer a mature person, fully equipped for good works (2 Tim. 3:16, 17). Before going further, pause for a few minutes and pray for the Holy Spirit to apply what you have studied thus far to your own life. Now list as many practical insights and applications as you can.

 FAITH ALIVE

Daniel said he was astonished at these visions. Yet "no one understood it." In other words, he did not tell other people about the visions nor try to explain why he had been sick (Dan. 7:28; 8:27).

"Wisdom is necessary to achieving one's full spiritual potential. The spiritually wise man knows when and when not to speak of things he has seen and heard and knows when and when not to pursue certain spiritual experiences."[7]

Some of God's secrets and visions are to be pondered and not proclaimed (Luke 2:19, 51). Sharing God's secrets unwisely or to gain the esteem of others may cause Him to withhold them from you in the future.

1. *Spirit-Filled Life Bible* (Nashville, TN: Thomas Nelson, Publishers, 1991), 1243, note on Daniel 7:1.

2. *The Believer's Study Bible* (Nashville, TN: Thomas Nelson, Publishers, 1991), 1192–1193, notes on Daniel 7:4–7.

3. *Spirit-Filled Life Bible*, 1245, "Kingdom Dynamics: Daniel 7:21, 22, Old Testament: Possessing the Kingdom."

4. *The Believer's Study Bible*, 1195, note on Daniel 8:8.

5. Ibid., note on Daniel 8:9.

6. *Spirit-Filled Life Bible*, 1246, notes on Daniel 8:9–14.

7. Ibid., 1254, "Truth-in-Action through Daniel," #4.

Lesson 5/ *The Restoration and Reward of Israel*
Daniel 9:1–27

Everyone likes a good mystery. The stimulus of the uncertain keeps us watching or reading. We want to discover how the conflicts will resolve, how the details will fit together, and how it will all end!

In Daniel's old age, he studied Scripture and sought the Lord to find out when the Jewish captivity in Babylon would be completed. He longed for the fulfillment of God's gracious promises to Israel. The account given us in chapter nine reveals God's destiny and timetable for the restoration of the Jews and Jerusalem.

From the prophecy of Jeremiah, who had prophesied to the Jews in Jerusalem before and during the deportations, Daniel observed that the "desolations of Jerusalem" would last a total of seventy years (Jer. 25:11; 29:10–14). Daniel realized he was nearing the completion of this prophetic period.

Later in this chapter, an angelic messenger revealed another mystery: after a set of sequences of yet another "seventy-sevens," the Messiah of Israel would establish the kingdom of God. At that time, the mysterious visions Daniel had received about the future—which has often been referred to as the "Times of the Gentiles"—would all be resolved and fulfilled.

DANIEL'S PRAYER FOR HIS PEOPLE
DANIEL 9:1–19

Daniel began his exile in 605 B.C. as a young man, first serving in the court of King Nebuchadnezzar. He continued to serve even after the Babylonian empire fell to the Medes and

Persians. Now in 538 B.C., during the greater rule of the Medo-Persian King Cyrus, we are told Darius was "made king over the realm of the Chaldeans" (Dan. 9:1). Daniel, after nearly seventy years in exile, continued to serve as a court advisor.

 FAITH ALIVE

The study of the prophecy of Jeremiah prompted Daniel to prayer. For the conscientious Christian, prophecy is neither escapism nor a distraction from current ministry. It is, instead, a high and holy motivation for the present. God the Father, Judge of heaven and earth, calls us to holiness, that we may escape the wrath to come (1 Thess. 1:9, 10). Sensitive understanding of prophecy prompts personal repentance and intercession for others.

How did Daniel show sincerity and godly sorrow as he interceded to God for his rebellious brothers? (v. 3)

Compare Daniel's actions to those of Jacob and Job in Genesis 37:31–35 and Job 42:5, 6.

How are fasting and prayer appropriate responses to prophecy?

How did Daniel acknowledge God's righteousness and Israel's sin?

Why did Daniel believe that his people were in exile? (Dan. 9:11)

According to the Law of Moses (Lev. 25:1–5), what was to happen in Israel every seven years?

According to Leviticus 26:33–35 this command was disobeyed and now the consequences had to be paid. How long would the Jews have to remain exiles in a foreign land?

The Babylonian captivity was not a fluke of history. Rather, it was a sovereignly enforced period for the land to "enjoy its Sabbaths" (Lev. 26:34). It was to compensate for the extended earlier violation of the Lord's Sabbath.

In Deuteronomy 30:1–3, 10, what did God tell the Jews they would need to do to be allowed to return to the land of Israel?

In Daniel 9:16–19, Daniel presented his petition to God:

Who was a reproach among the people?

Who was known to be merciful?

Whose reputation was at stake?

THE SEVENTY-WEEK PROPHECY
DANIEL 9:20–27

In response to Daniel's penitent prayer and fasting, God sent His archangel Gabriel, giving Daniel an enigmatic answer that is one of the most critical prophetic passages in Scripture. Some of the predicted events have since been fulfilled with literal precision, and others—which are yet to come—provide the framework for the end times.

 BEHIND THE SCENES

Gabriel's prophecy is about the coming and crucifixion of Christ, when He would make an end of transgressions and sins and reconcile man to God. But his kingdom of "everlasting righteousness" has not come to full power, and the "most Holy" has not yet been anointed.

The Old Testament prophets didn't see the double fulfillment of the coming of the Messiah (Eph. 3:3–7). When Jesus read the scriptures in the synagogue in His hometown of Nazareth, He stopped halfway through the selected section of Isaiah (Is. 61) and said, "Today this scripture is fulfilled in your hearing" (Luke 4:16–21). He did not read the complete passage because only the first half concerned His first coming. The "day of vengeance" (Is. 61:2b) belongs to His Second Coming.

How many periods of weeks (literally "sevens") are determined for Daniel's people and the holy city of Jerusalem? (9:24)

PROBING THE DEPTHS

The following chart from *The Believer's Study Bible* displays a dispensational understanding of Daniel's seventy weeks:

The Prophecy of Seventy Weeks (490 Years)[1]					
Decree of Artaxerxes to Nehemiah—March 14, 445 B.C.		Presentation of Messiah as Prince—April 6, A.D. 32	Covenant of Antichrist with Israel		Return of Messiah to Establish Kingdom of God
v. 25 Sixty-nine Weeks (483 Years)		v. 26 Gap of Time		v. 27 Seventieth Week	
(Seven Weeks) 49 Years to Complete Rebuilding of Jerusalem	(Sixty-two Weeks= 434 Years)	Messiah Cut Off—A.D. 33 / Jerusalem and Sanctuary Destroyed—A.D. 70	Image of Antichrist in Temple	3½ Years	3½ Years Desolation by Antichrist / Six Purposes v. 24

However, students of the classical (non-dispensational) approach to prophetic interpretation do not view the value expressed by the phrase "seventy weeks" literally, as referring precisely to 490 years. Adherents note that nowhere are the "weeks" (literally "sevens") said to be years. Instead, such students understand Daniel's use of "seventy weeks" in much the same way as they understand Jesus' use of "seventy times seven" when He instructs Peter to forgive freely (Matt. 18:21, 22). It is clear that Jesus intends Peter to forgive generously, without thought of tallying instances of forgiveness, only to refuse to forgive at offense #491. Students of the classical view of prophecy see Daniel's use of "seventy weeks" similarly, as referring to a very long, indefinite period in which Israel is punished for her transgressions. In any case, however:

What are stated as the six main purposes for this period? (Dan. 9:24)

When does God's prophetic clock begin ticking? (See v. 25.)

AT A GLANCE

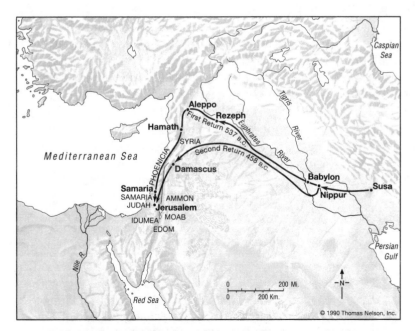

The Return from Exile. When Cyrus the Persian captured Babylon in 539 B.C., the way was opened for captive Judah to begin the return to her homeland. Two major expeditions made the journey, one in 537 B.C. and another in 458 B.C.[2]

Why did God's messenger divide the sixty-nine weeks into two parts? (Dan. 9:24–27)

The seventy-sevens are divided into three sections: seven, sixty-two, and one. The first section of sevens was to be measured from the time a decree would be given to "restore and rebuild Jerusalem." This is thought to have been done on March 14, 445 B.C. by the Medo-Persian ruler, Artaxerxes Longimanus (see Neh. 2:5).

Those who use this date believe the complete sixty-nine weeks came to an end when Christ made his Triumphal Entry into Jerusalem as Israel's Messiah on Palm Sunday (Ps. 118:22–26; Luke 19:28–44; Rom. 8:22, 23; Zech. 9:9). Four-hundred-eighty-three prophetic years of 360 days each is equal to 173,880 days. This was calculated by Sir Robert Anderson as being *exactly* the period between March 14, 445 B.C. and April 6, A.D. 32, counting the period between 1 B.C. and A.D. 1 as one year. This date would have been Palm Sunday, when Jesus was rejected as the Messiah by national Israel! Amazing![3]

Others see the sixty-two-week cycle beginning in 457 B.C. and concluding 483 years later when Jesus was baptized by John in the Jordan River (see Luke 3:22, 23). They suggest that since Jesus received his "anointing" with the Holy Spirit at that time and began "preaching the gospel of the kingdom of God, and saying, The time is fulfilled" that it was then that God recognized him as the "Messiah" or the anointed one.

WORD WEALTH

Messiah, *mashiach* (mah-*shee*-ahch); *Strong's* #4899: Anointed one, messiah. Found 39 times in the Old Testament, *mashiach* is derived from the verb *mashach,* "to anoint," "to consecrate by applying the holy anointing oil to an individual." *Mashiach* describes the high priest (Lev. 4:3, 16) and anointed kings, such as Saul (2 Sam. 1:14) and David (2 Sam. 19:21; Ps. 18:50). In Ps. and in Dan. *mashiach* is particularly used for

David's anointed heir, the king of Israel and ruler of all nations
(see Ps. 2:2; 28:8, Dan. 9:25, 26). When the earliest followers
of Jesus spoke of Him, they called Him Jesus the Messiah, or
in Hebrew, *Yeshua ha-Mashiach.* "Messiah" or "Anointed One"
is *Christos* in Greek and is the origin of the English form
"Christ." Whenever the Lord is called "Jesus Christ," He is
being called "Jesus the Messiah."[4]

The prophecy said that the Messiah, which can be translated "Anointed One," was to be abruptly "cut off" without
receiving His share of the kingdom (Dan. 9:26). The first 483
years of Daniel's prophecy culminated with the crucifixion of the
Lord Jesus Christ in Jerusalem, the "city of our God."

From the very beginning of our Lord's earthly existence
He was closely linked with Jerusalem and the temple there. He
made seven recorded visits to the capital city, each with special
interest in the temple.

  ## BEHIND THE SCENES

"Five temples are significant in the Jewish story:
1. Solomon's temple, (c. 1000 B.C.), symbol of Israel's glorious past; **2. Zerubbabel's temple,** (c. 536 B.C.), a vastly infe-
rior structure constructed by the Jews upon their return from
the Babylonian captivity; **3. Herod's temple,** begun around 19
B.C., to replace Zerubbabel's building. It was a magnificent edifice in service in Jesus' day, but destroyed by Titus in A.D. 70;
4. Antichrist's temple, built either before or during the early
part of the first 3½ years of the tribulation, but due to be
destroyed by the final earthquake before Jesus returns;
5. Jesus Christ's temple, built at the beginning of the millennium for Jesus' 1,000-year reign on earth."[5]

According to Daniel 9:25, how many weeks are to pass
from the time of the decree to restore and rebuild Jerusalem
until the coming of the Messiah?

What two features are mentioned in Daniel 9:26 as occurring *after* the sixty-ninth week?

How did the destruction of the city and temple by Titus in A.D. 70 possibly fulfill this phase of the prophecy?

Compare "the prince who is to come" with the beast from the sea in Daniel 8 and the "little horn" of 7:8.

 BIBLE EXTRA

This final seven-year period in Daniel's seventy weeks is commonly known among futurist interpreters as the "Great Tribulation" because of the suffering and severe testing which is to be endured by those living on the earth at that time. Classical interpreters, however, see the initial fulfillment of Daniel's prophetic sections in past historical events, with the ultimate fulfillment for many prophecies to be experienced at the end of this age.

This final period of the "times of the Gentiles" is projected by futurists to begin when the Antichrist makes a covenant to protect Israel for a seven-year period (Is. 28:14–17). The first half of that time (42 months; Rev. 13:1–5) will be known to the Jews as "the beginning of sorrows" (Matt. 24:8). It will be characterized by conquest, war, famine, persecution, and death (Matt. 24:6–12; Rev. 6:1–8), as the Antichrist gathers a coalition of nations under his power and persuasion (Rev. 13:3–5).

However, in the middle of Daniel's Seventieth Week (after 3½ years), the Antichrist will change his stance toward the Jews and demand that they worship him. This is the "abomination of desolation" to which Daniel and Paul refer (Dan. 9:27; 2 Thess. 2:2–4). It is followed by the period known as the "Great Tribulation" (Matt. 24:21, 29; Mark 13:19, 24; Rev. 7:14). It will include the desecration of the temple, great persecution of Israel, and the more severe judgments of the Tribulation period as God pours out His wrath (Rev. 6:17).

The final seven-year period concludes "after the tribulation of those days" with the Second Coming of Jesus, the Messiah (Matt. 24:29–31; Rev. 19:11–21). Following those events, Jesus will set up His kingdom and reign with His saints on earth for 1,000 years (Rev. 20:4–6), and then for all eternity with a new heaven, a new earth, and a new Jerusalem (Rev. 21).

 FAITH ALIVE

Regardless of which prophetic approach most convinces us, what difference should this study of end-times prophecy make in our lives? How should we live as we await the Lord's return?

Romans 13:11–14 emphasizes a high standard of moral conduct, especially in view of the nearness of Christ's return. Read this passage and then comment on Paul's two calls for moral excellence, one he states positively (something we should do) and one negatively (something we should not do).

The Positive:

The Negative:

For each, note how you are doing in your life now:

1. *The Believer's Study Bible* (Nashville, TN: Thomas Nelson, Publishers, 1991), 1198.
2. *Spirit-Filled Life Bible* (Nashville, TN: Thomas Nelson Publishers, 1991), 659.
3. Sir Robert Anderson, *The Coming Prince* (Grand Rapids, MI: Kregel, 1977), 127.
4. *Spirit-Filled Life Bible*, 1249, "Word Wealth: Daniel 9:25, Messiah."
5. C. S. Lovett, *Latest Word on the Last Days* (Baldwin Park, CA: Personal Christianity Chapel, 1980), 134.

Lesson 6/ World History Revealed
Daniel 10:1—12:13

Daniel 10—12 contains one great unit of prophecy revealing world history in advance. Two years before this final vision given to Daniel in 538 B.C., the Persian King, Cyrus, had issued a decree allowing some of the exiled Jews to return to Jerusalem to rebuild the house of God (2 Chron. 36:22, 23; Ezra 1; Is. 44:28). Now, after this brief time, Daniel either has been told of, or senses in his spirit, the opposition and resistance his people were facing in rebuilding the temple in Jerusalem.

VISIONS OF THE GLORIOUS MAN
DANIEL 10:1–9

Daniel 10:2, 3 reveals the prophet's temporary abstinence from certain foods, which reflects what some call a "Daniel's fast." He went without pastries, meat, and wine as a discipline to express spiritual mourning. Some have suggested that this three-week fast was during the period of the Passover Feast.

During this fast, Daniel saw a vision of a man (Dan. 10:5). How is he described?

Compare Daniel's description with the description of Jesus in Revelation 1:12–16.

How did Daniel react to this vision? (Dan. 10:5, 6) How is this like others who found themselves in the presence of God? (See Is. 6:1–5; Luke 5:8.)

Daniel 10:10 seems to introduce an additional personality to the vision. What is the reason for his presence?

What difficulty did the angelic messenger encounter in reaching Daniel? (Dan. 10:13)

Who withstood Michael from coming to Daniel? (v. 13)

What do verses 12 and 13 tell us about spiritual conflict in the invisible realm?

How do these two passages of scripture explain why—in certain cases—there are delays in the answer to our prayers?

Once we understand the reality of spiritual conflict in the invisible realm, what should be our role as intercessors and prayer warriors in partnering with the Holy Spirit to win victories for Jesus Christ?

What role does perservering prayer have in spiritual conflict?

PROBING THE DEPTHS

Daniel 10:13 provides one of the clearest Old Testament examples that demonic armies oppose God's purposes and that earthly struggles often reflect what is happening in the heavenlies, and that prayer with fasting may affect the outcome. **The prince of . . . Persia** would be the head of the spiritual forces marshaled on behalf of sinful Persia, especially in relation to its destructive interaction with God's people. Michael is a senior angel. The exact nature of the conflict and why the messenger could not defeat the prince are not stated."[1]

It would appear that the demonic world is exceedingly active in the affairs of nations and national issues. The conflict is *in* the spiritual realm, yet it is *expressed through* political, military, and other realms.

How should a spiritually enlightened understanding of this fact affect our prayers for governmental leaders? (See Dan. 10:20, 21 and 1 Tim. 2:1–4 before answering.)

FAITH ALIVE

There is a constant struggle in the spiritual world over the control of people's lives. How do the following verses indicate that we are able to bind the works and powers of the enemy and to battle for God's side?

Matt. 16:19

2 Cor. 10:4

Eph. 6:12

What is our responsibility as intercessors and prayer warriors in exercising this kingdom authority?

What can happen if we do not assume our role as intercessors?

PROPHECIES CONCERNING PERSIA AND GREECE
DANIEL 11:2–35

Daniel 11 appears to prophesy the plight of the Jews and the suffering they will endure in the centuries to follow. They will continue in danger throughout modern history and until the end of the Great Tribulation.

From a twentieth-century vantage point all prophecy in Daniel up to 11:35 can be related to well-known events of ancient history. For instance, the dreams Daniel interpreted in chapters 2, 7, and 8 overlap in meaning and relate to features of the Babylonian, Medo-Persian, Greek, and Roman world empires.

Daniel 11:2–4 describes again Alexander's rise and the future division of his empire between his four generals (Ptolemy, Seleucus 1, Cassander, and Lysimachus) after Alexander was cut off in his prime at age thirty-three. Daniel 11:5–20 predicts the intrigue and struggles between Egypt and Syria right up until the time of Antiochus Epiphanes (c. 175–164 B.C.). Daniel 11:21–35 describes the outrageous actions of Antiochus and ultimately of the final enemy of God's people, the Antichrist.

THE NORTHERN KING'S BLASPHEMIES AND CONQUESTS
DANIEL 11:36–45

The remaining verses of Daniel 11 reveal features of "the time of the end" (vv. 35, 40).

What suggests that the Antichrist will be obsessed with military force? Compare this to Ezekiel 38:8, 9, 11, and 16.

As fierce as the Antichrist may be, he will not prevail against the true Christ, the Anointed One of God. What will be his eventual end? (See Rev. 19:11–21.)

PROPHECY OF THE END TIME
DANIEL 12:1–13

So severe, however, will be the agonizing days of God's wrath, predicted in Daniel 9:27 and revealed further in Revelation 16 that, except for the restraining work of the archangel Michael (Dan. 12:1), Israel's guardian angel, the remaining human race might face annihilation (Matt. 24:22).

How do Michael and his angels fight against Satan and his angels? (See Rev. 12:7–9.)

Daniel distinguishes two phases of a future resurrection of the dead (Dan. 2:2). Some will be resurrected to everlasting life and some to shame and everlasting contempt or abhorrence. The former most likely refers to the "last days" resurrection of the remnant of Jewish martyrs (Rev. 6:9; Matt. 10:22, 23) which precedes the Great White Throne Judgment after the Millennium.

How are these future events separated in Revelation 20:4–6?

How does Daniel refer to these faithful martyrs? (Dan. 12:3)

Daniel is ordered to conceal and close up the book until "the time of the end" (Dan. 12:4, 9). When the end time comes, the church will have a greater historical perspective to understand prophecy. In the view of many, since Israel regained control of its homeland (1948), and of the city of Jerusalem (1967), we have a much clearer perspective on prophecy because the end time is significantly nearer than before.

 ### FAITH ALIVE

Throughout the history of the church, many Christians have become so consumed with the future realities that they have neglected their present responsibilities. For instance, during the first century A.D. believers in Thessalonica heard that Christ had already come and established His kingdom on earth (2 Thess. 2:2). Some of them used this news to excuse themselves from work and to engage in gossip (2 Thess. 3:11, 12). After challenging their response to this unfounded message (vv. 14, 15), the apostle Paul corrected their theology, reminding them of what he had taught them about the last days (2 Thess. 2:3–12).

How are you handling your own priorities until the end of time?

With the prospect of these awful afflictions and challenging circumstances near "the time of the end," how are the wise and righteous to respond? (2 Thess. 1:10)

1. *Spirit-Filled Life Bible* (Nashville, TN: Thomas Nelson Publishers, 1991), 1250, note on Daniel 10:13.
2. Ibid., 1252, notes on Daniel 11:36–45.

Lesson 7/The Letters to the Seven Churches
Revelation 1:1—3:22

What will happen in the final years of this world's history?

God is the only one with an answer to such a question. Mankind can only know what the future holds if God chooses to reveal or "unveil" the answers.

The Book of Revelation is such an "unveiling" of supernatural wisdom and destiny. It is typically apocalyptic (Gr. *apokalupsis,* meaning "disclosure" or "uncovering") in form, containing much figurative description, with an abundance of symbolism and prophecies in regard to the future. What the Book of Daniel is to the Old Testament, the Book of Revelation is to the New Testament.

 BIBLE EXTRA

Read through the entire Book of Revelation at one sitting. It only takes about one hour. Don't try to analyze every detail the first time, but try to understand the general flow of thought. Read it again, marking its main divisions. Seek to understand its message, not every sign and symbol: Neither *Who*? nor *When*?, but *What is the basic concept*? should be your main consideration.

Read about Revelation in a Bible dictionary or encyclopedia. Read the articles on the seven churches of Revelation 2 and 3. The articles will help you understand the culture in which the churches existed and enable you to compare them to today's culture and churches.

THE REVELATION OF JESUS CHRIST
REVELATION 1:1–3

From the beginning of this book (Rev. 1:1) we note that this revelation is of Jesus Christ Himself. It is an unveiling of His plans (Rev. 1:19) for His creation, His church, and the community of His people in "a new heaven and a new earth" (Rev. 21:1).

What are stated as the source and purpose of the book? (Rev. 1:1, 2)

Who is the author, the one relating the revelation? (v. 1)

    BIBLE EXTRA

Note this background information on Revelation:

"**Author:** Four times the author refers to himself as 'John' (Rev. 1:1, 4, 9; 22:8). He was so well known to his readers, and his spiritual authority was so widely acknowledged, that he did not need to establish his credentials. Early church tradition unanimously attributed this book to the apostle John.

"**Background and Date:** Evidence within Revelation indicates that it was written during a period of extreme persecution of Christians, which possibly was that begun by Nero after the great fire that nearly destroyed Rome in July of A.D. 64 and continued until his suicide in June of A.D. 68. In this view, the book was thus written before the destruction of Jerusalem in September of A.D. 70, and is an authentic prophecy concerning the continuing suffering and persecution of Christians, which would become even more intense and severe in the years ahead. On the basis of isolated statements by the early church fathers, some interpreters date the book near the end of the reign of Domitian (A.D. 81–96), after John had fled to Ephesus."[1]

FAITH ALIVE

This book of Scripture is unique in that it contains a promise of blessing to its readers: "Blessed is he who *reads* and those who *hear* the words of this prophecy, and keep those things which are written in it; for the time is near" (emphasis added, Rev. 1:3).

The Greek word *makarios* is translated as "blessed." This word is found seven times in Revelation (1:3; 14:13; 16:15; 19:9; 20:6; 22:7,14). It is the familiar word used by our Lord in the Beatitudes in Matthew 5 and Luke 6, where it indicates not only the characters that are blessed, but also the nature of that which is the highest good.

The Lord pronounces those who *read, hear,* and *keep* the words of this prophecy as "happy, fulfilled, and satisfied." They have this inner satisfaction because God dwells within them, not necessarily because of favorable circumstances. The blessing of God can bring peace in the middle of turmoil and the storms of life.

The kingdom of God is "within" and among us. May His kingdom's rule in our lives and the hope of heaven in our spirits draw others to the kingdom, "for the time is near."

GOD'S FINAL MESSAGE
REVELATION 1:4–11

The Revelation was addressed (v. 4) and sent (v. 11) to the Seven Churches of Asia Minor (now the country of Turkey) which are mentioned in chapters two and three. In this prologue, the apostle gives the salutation (vv. 4–8), and then states the circumstances surrounding his Patmos vision.

Trace the steps of transmission of the Revelation from God to us using verses 1, 2, 4, 10, and 11.

The book is filled with doxologies of praise to God and His Son Jesus, our Lord. Verses 5 and 6 exalt the Lord Jesus Christ for who He is and what He has done. Delineate each below:

Who He is:

What He has done:

WORD WEALTH

Witness, *martus* (mar-*toos*); Strong's *#3144.* Compare 'martyr' and 'martyrdom.' One who testifies to the truth he has experienced, a witness, one who has knowledge of a fact and can give information concerning it. The word in itself does not imply death, but many of the first-century witnesses did give their lives, with the result that the word came to denote a martyr, one who witnesses for Christ by his death (Acts 22:20; Rev. 2:13; 17:6).[2]

PROBING THE DEPTHS

"**Worship and the Kingdom.** In the opening of Revelation, John introduces himself as a brother and companion in the struggle we all face (Rev. 1:9). His words 'in the kingdom and patience of Jesus Christ' point to the dual facts of Christ's present kingdom triumph and the ongoing presence of evil and warfare that exact the patience of the church in the kingdom advances among and through us. In prefacing the broad arenas of prophecy about to be unfolded, John addresses two very important *present* truths: (1) We, Christ's redeemed, are loved and are washed from our sins—a present state (Rev. 1:5). (2) We, through His glorious dominion, have been designated 'kings and priests' to God—also a present calling. Thus, these dual offices give perspective on our authority and duty and how we most effectively may advance the kingdom of God.

"First, we are said to be kings in the sense that under the King of kings we are the new breed—the reborn, to whom God has delegated authority to extend and administrate the powers of His rule. Of course, this involves faithful witness to the gospel in the power of the Spirit and loving service to humanity in the love of God. But it also involves confrontation with dark powers of hell, assertive prayer warfare, and an expectation of the miraculous works of God (2 Cor. 10:3–5; Eph. 6:10–20; 1 Cor. 2:4). However, this authority is only fully accomplished in the spirit of praiseful worship, as we exercise the office of 'priests.' Some translations read, 'a kingdom of priests,' which emphasizes that the rule is only effective when the priestly mission is faithfully attended. Worship is foundational to kingdom advance. The power of the believer before God's throne, worshiping the Lamb and exalting in the Holy Spirit of praise, is mightily confounding to the Adversary. See Ex. 19:5–7, Ps. 22:3; 93:2; 1 Pet. 2:9)"[3]

Revelation 1:7 says that when Jesus Christ returns in judgment at the Second Coming (see Zech. 12:10; Matt. 24:30) "every eye shall see him." How could this be possible?

How might modern communications technology contribute to this?

"The Alpha and the Omega" are the first and last letters of the Greek alphabet, like "A to Z" in the English alphabet and idiom. This descriptive term indicates that He is the eternal Lord of all (Is. 44:6), the beginning and the end of all things (Rev. 1:17). God started it and will end it when He is ready.

 BEHIND THE SCENES

"John is an exile on Patmos, an island ten miles by six miles, located sixty miles southwest of Ephesus in the Aegean

Sea. Volcanic and mostly treeless, the Romans used it as a penal colony, forcing prisoners to work in the granite quarries. John's banishment was the result of his faithful witness to the gospel."[4]

What kind of tribulation/persecution are you facing? None of us escapes it. John identified with us (Rev. 1:9) as our "brother and companion in . . . tribulation. . . ." Though he was on a barren island and in bleak circumstances he was to be uniquely used of God. How may that encourage us?

Revelation 1:10 "is the earliest reference in Christian literature to the first day of the week as *the Lord's Day*."[5] This apparently became the day of the week early Christians observed as their day of rest and worship. (See Acts 20:7; 1 Cor. 16:2.) It should be noted that observance of the Jewish Sabbath is neither commanded nor condemned in the New Testament. (See Acts 15:1, 24; Rom. 14:5, 6.)

THE RISEN CHRIST
REVELATION 1:12–20

Many believers only think of the suffering Jesus hanging on the cross. But John saw the Son of Man as an awesome Being (see Rev. 1:13–16) and fell at His feet, as though he were dead (Rev. 1:17). If we had a true glimpse of Christ's majesty, holiness, and power, perhaps we too would fall down worship Him "in spirit and in truth." Perhaps the brilliance of His glory would reveal areas and aspects of our lives for which we need quick and genuine repentance!

The Lord Jesus came from heaven to earth to redeem mankind. He willingly left His royal glory behind to become a servant to His creatures on earth (Phil. 2:6–11). But now, having risen from the grave, He has returned to heaven and the glory He set aside for us. In Revelation 1:13–16, John shares with us his glimpse of godly glory.

Revelation 1:19 presents a simple outline of Revelation: (1) "the things you have seen," (those things John had just beheld in his initial encounter with the glorified Lord); (2) "the things which are," (Revelation 2 and 3, relating about existing churches in the Roman province of Asia which represented the church throughout the entire church age); and (3) "the things which shall take place after this," speaking of those things to come after that time.

Revelation 1:20 continues the symbolism used in the book. Seven stars and seven lampstands are identified and explained: "The seven stars are the angels of the seven churches, and the seven lampstands which you saw are the seven churches."

Who are the angels of the seven churches? (Rev. 1:20) Are they supernatural guardians or human leaders of the local churches?

In what place of prominence and protection did the Son of Man hold the seven stars? (Rev. 1:16)

What is represented by "the seven golden lampstands"? (Rev. 1:20)

BIBLE EXTRA

The *King James Version* consistently translates the word *luchnos(nia)* as "candle" or "candlestick." All modern translations give the more literal "lamp" or "lampstand." The difference is significant: a candle will burn and consume itself; the lamp contains oil and a wick and can continue to burn and give light if its oil is replenished and its wick consistently trimmed.

What does this say about spiritual renewal and holy living in the local church?

It is of interest that the lamps are not described as physically united—as in the seven-branched Jewish menorah. Rather they are related because they have the same Owner. How does this relate to spiritual unity in the body of Christ?

If shape and form of the lampstands are not issues, what does this say to us about diversity in forms of worship and styles of services?

In the message to the church at Ephesus, Jesus said that He "walks in the midst of the seven golden lampstands" (2:1). This seems to suggest an **intimate concern** and **intense care** for the local assemblies of believers. He is the One who fills (and refills) the oil, and trims (and even replaces) the wick. What could this suggest about spiritual renewal and leadership in a local church?

Do you need more "oil in your lamp"? Do you need your wick trimmed? Are you "burned out"?

AT A GLANCE

THE SEVEN CHURCHES OF THE APOCALYPSE (1:20)[8]			
	Commendation	**Criticism**	**Instruction**	**Promise**
Ephesus (2:1–7)	Rejects evil, perseveres, has patience	Love for Christ no longer fervent	Do the works you did at first	The tree of life
Smyrna (2:8–11)	Gracefully bears suffering	None	Be faithful until death	The crown of life
Pergamos (2:12–17)	Keeps the faith of Christ	Tolerates immorality, idolatry, and heresies	Repent	Hidden manna and a stone with a new name
Thyatira (2:18–29)	Love, service, faith, patience is greater than at first	Tolerates cult of idolatry and immorality	Judgment coming; keep the faith	Rule over nations and receive morning star
Sardis (3:1–6)	Some have kept the faith	A dead church	Repent; strengthen what remains	Faithful honored and clothed in white
Philadelphia (3:7–13)	Perseveres in the faith	None	Keep the faith	A place in God's presence, a new name, and the New Jerusalem
Laodicea (3:14–22)	None	Indifferent	Be zealous and repent	Share Christ's throne

These letters show what different groups of believers will do in times of persecution. The churches were specific congregations in John's day, but they also are representative of similar types of churches, regardless of place or time.

In these epistles the risen Lord administers His church. Each letter includes:

- an accusation or commendation,
- a call or directive, and
- a threat or a promise.

Though they were *actual churches,* they also seem to have been selected as *parable churches* to give us heavenly instruction as we would apply the principles throughout all generations of the church (Rev. 2:7, 11, 17, 29; 3:6, 13, 22).

EPHESUS: THE LOVELESS CHURCH
REVELATION 2:1–7

The church in Ephesus was one of the leading congregations in Asia Minor. It probably came about as a result of Paul's brief ministry there on his second journey (Acts 18:18–21). The church was firmly established during Paul's extended stay on his third journey (Acts 19:1, 2, 6, 8–12, 20). His epistle to the Ephesians is rich in truth and doctrine, as well as guidance for practical Christian living.

In Revelation 2:2, what four things did He say had not gone unnoticed?

John also observed that they had faithfully practiced church discipline by not enduring the professed Christian who persisted in practicing sin.

SMYRNA: THE PERSECUTED CHURCH
REVELATION 2:8–11

Another leading congregation in Asia Minor was located in the town of Smyrna, about forty miles north of Ephesus. Of the seven cities addressed in Revelation 2 and 3, this is the only one which exists today; it is the modern Turkish town of Izmir. In the first century it was a wealthy seaport, and a place of advanced culture for that time. In A.D. 23 it had won the privilege from the Roman Senate to build the first temple in honor of the Roman emperor, Tiberius. That set the stage for the politically-correct practice of emperor worship.

Christ affirmed that He was well aware of four aspects of their faithful endurance (Rev. 2:9). Name them:

Though they were persecuted by unbelieving and hostile Jews, who was the true source of their troubles? (v. 9b)

FAITH ALIVE

Who can deny that we—as Christians—have troubles, pressures, or "tribulations"? The word in Revelation 1:9 which is translated "tribulations" (Gr. *thlipsis*) was also used in classical Greek to describe the way the Romans would torture someone by applying the pressure of heavy stones to the chest of a criminal. This heavy pressure had the effect of slowly mashing the individual to death.

Do you have problems that are "slowly mashing" you down to the point you feel you can't take it any more? Emotionally, do you feel lonely and depressed? Financially, are you falling so far behind you despair? Physically, have you had ill health or bad medical test results? Spiritually, are you filled with doubt or guilt? Jesus says he "knows" all about our afflictions, our deep distresses, our pressing problems. He knows and cares! He knows our present pressures and future trials as well. His Word assures us of final victory (Rom. 8:31–39)!

Christ prophesied of a time of intense future persecution for the believers in Smyrna. Satan, he said, would actually deliver many of them into prison. In the face of this dour prediction, what were they told to be?

What did He promise to give to those who were faithful unto death? Compare this with James 1:12 and 1 Peter 5:4.

The apostle Paul told Timothy that "all who desire to live godly in Christ Jesus will suffer persecution" (2 Tim. 3:12). As a matter of fact, there may well come a time in the near future when it will be common for Christians to again be martyred for their beliefs.

In his Gospel, John said that some who persecute the church will do so because of an odd conviction. What was it? (See John 16:2.)

Does death separate us from God? (See Rom. 8:35–39; 2 Cor. 5:1–8.)

What did the Lord say His followers would not be harmed by? (See Rev. 2:11, and compare with Rev. 20:6, 14; 21:8 and Daniel 12:2.)

PERGAMOS: THE COMPROMISING CHURCH
REVELATION 2:12–17

About sixty-five miles north of Smyrna lay the beautiful inland city of Pergamos. It was the oldest city in the province and capital of Roman Asia. Its library is said to have contained over 200,000 volumes of parchment scrolls. The library was later given as a gift from Mark Anthony to Cleopatra.

Pergamos was obviously a hostile and difficult place for Christian believers to live—"where Satan has his throne." The oppressive force of demonic powers was all around. The culture of the community was so given to pagan gods and emperor worship that Antipas, apparently one of the believers in Pergamos, had become the first Christian in Asia to be martyred for his faith.

How did the believers respond in these difficult situations? (Rev. 2:13)

What suggests the strong public testimony given by this church? (Rev. 2:13)

In spite of its strengths, Christ identified two serious flaws in the church's beliefs and behavior (Rev. 2:14). His accusations surrounded the fact that they had become broadminded about the "narrow way." Some had been snared by Satan and surrendered to the teaching and practice of the Balaamites and the Nicolaitans, which Christ said he *hates* (Rev. 2:6). Their spiritual compromises short-circuited their spiritual effectiveness.

BIBLE EXTRA

In Numbers 25, Balak, the king of Moab, cannot succeed in getting the old prophet Balaam to curse Israel directly. But Balaam, apparently for personal profit, does deceive God's people and devise a plan whereby the daughters of the Moabites seduce the Israelite men and entice them to sin and sacrifice to their god—Baal-peor—and worship him. God's judgment falls on Israel because of their fornication and idolatry. (Additionally see Num. 31:16; 2 Pet. 2:15; Jude 11.)

Another deadly doctrine condemned by Christ is that of the Nicolaitans. This radical sect of hedonistic heretics followed an extreme form of Gnosticism rampant throughout the first century. "Supporters of this deadly doctrine claimed that, since their bodies were physical (and therefore evil), only what their spirits did was important. So they felt free to indulge in indiscriminate sexual relationships, to eat food which had been offered to idols, and to do anything they pleased with their bodies."[9]

Christ clearly called this compromising church to "repent, or else . . ." (Rev. 2:16). The term means to change your mind or way of thinking (and thus your way of living!). God does not want His people to hold liberal, lenient attitudes toward religious idolatry and sexual promiscuity. These behaviors are clearly condemned in God's Word and must be avoided in our lives and fellowship. If they are not, God will do what He needs to do to purge evil from His church (Heb. 12:6).

How can we avoid being "narrow minded" and yet not tolerate sin?

Paul told the Christians in Thessalonica (1 Thess. 4:1–8) that God's will for our lives involved at least three things relating to our bodies. What are they?

1.

2.

3.

Paul told the Roman Christians we should avoid certain premeditated plans (Rom. 13:14). What are they?

To avoid compromise and overcome sinful temptation, certain spiritual discernment is needed. This comes to mature believers who feed on the meat of the Word and not just on the milk. Their spiritual senses are able to discriminate between sound and unsound doctrine and between wholesome and unwholesome conduct. (See Heb. 5:12–14.)

THYATIRA: THE CORRUPT CHURCH
REVELATION 2:18–29

Thyatira was about thirty-five miles southeast of Pergamos. It had been founded nearly 400 years before by Alexander the Great. Lydia, Paul's first convert in Europe, came from this town (Acts 16:14) as a businesswoman selling the popular purple fabric made in Thyatira.

The church of that city was in serious trouble, caused by the demands of the many trade guilds (such as tanners, potters, weavers, dyers, and robe makers). These fraternal associations frequently sponsored ceremonial feasts that featured food "sacrificed" to some pagan deity, possibly the guild's patron god. Moreover, the immoral conduct which often characterized such occasions made it impossible for genuine Christians to participate in the guild or its activities.

What parallel may there be between these ancient guilds and modern trade unions or fraternal organizations?

What immorality or religious-like (non-Christian) behavior accompanies such secular meetings and activities, if any?

While matters like the eating of food sacrificed to idols need hardly worry us today in Western society, the principle here is as important and relevant as ever: Do we take our standards from contemporary moral values or from God's unchanging Word?

The Thyatiran letter is all about Christian life and witness in a permissive society. What kind of similar issues do you see in your city and society?

What are some of your personal convictions which, like good policy, predetermine how you will respond when faced unexpectedly with moral issues?

FAITH ALIVE

Consider the following principles and questions to help in developing your own personal convictions. Objectively apply *all* the following 'guidelines for gray areas' to a given issue before deciding if the matter in question is right or wrong for you.

1. **Profit** (1 Cor. 6:12). Ask the questions: 'Is it good for me?' 'Will it add a plus quality to my life?'
2. **Control** (1 Cor. 6:12). Ask the questions: 'Will it get control of me, or will it lessen Christ's control of me?'
3. **Ownership** (1 Cor. 6:19, 20). Consider the questions: 'As God's property, can I justify this activity? Is this activity befitting an ambassador of Jesus Christ?'
4. **Influence** (1 Cor. 8:9, 12, 13). Consider: 'Could this action negatively influence any of my friends or cause them to stumble?'
5. **Testimony** (Col. 4:5). Now consider: 'How will my testimony be affected if I participate in this activity?'
6. **Thanksgiving** (Col. 3:17). Reflect on this question: 'When I come home from this activity, can I thank God for it with a clear conscience?'
7. **Love** (Rom. 14:13–15). As the final question ask: 'Am I willing to limit my liberties, in loving consideration of another?'[10]

Christ offered the saints His fivefold commendation (Rev. 2:19). What positive things did He single out?

What was God's main objection with this congregation?

What was projected as punishment for the contemporary prophetess, named Jezebel, and her followers?

How would her punishment serve as an example to other churches?

After warning the wayward, how did Christ encourage the saints?

SARDIS: THE DEAD CHURCH
REVELATION 3:1–6

Thirty miles southeast of Thyatira and fifty miles due east of Smyrna, was Sardis, a city renowned for its dyeing process and woolen industries.

In this series of letters the pattern had been for Christ to offer a commendation to the congregation before stating His condemnation. However, in this letter to the church in Sardis any praise is missing. Instead, harsh evaluation is immediate. The problem was not sensuality, but spirituality. Here was a spiritually weak congregation living off the accolades of their past. Their spiritual service to Christ was in another day. Now they were nothing. They had a history, and reveled in their reputation, but for the most part the current congregation had one foot in the grave (Rev. 3:1, 4). They no doubt sang hymns together, prayed together, gave, taught, and talked together, yet they were declared "dead."

The situation was dire, but not totally hopeless. If quick and decisive steps were taken, some people and the church's ministry could be salvaged. What five things did Christ command them to do? (Rev. 3:2, 3)

1.

2.

3.

4.

5.

What caution or warning did Christ give concerning their failure to do as He directed them? (Rev. 3:3b)

Those who demonstrated their spiritual sincerity would be rewarded by Christ's daily companionship ("walk with me") and consequent purity ("in white"; Rev. 3:4). What three things are promised to the one who overcomes? (Rev. 3:5)

1.

2.

3.

What warnings about spiritual senility can you glean from this letter?

Inflexibility suggests something which is dead. Living things are pliable. What ways of thinking and living may God be calling you to change in order to conform to Christ?

PHILADELPHIA: THE FAITHFUL CHURCH
REVELATION 3:7–13

The name "philadelphia" means "brotherly love," and the word is used (in slightly different forms) seven other times in the New Testament to refer to this beautiful Christian attribute. Two prime examples are:

"Be kindly affectionate to one another with brotherly love, in honor giving preference to one another" (Rom. 12:10).

"Let brotherly love continue . . ." (Heb. 13:1).

Nothing is known about the origin of the church in Philadelphia. The city itself was built by the king of Pergamos in honor of his brother. Its location on a major highway connecting several of the key cities of that area helped establish Philadelphia as a strong fortress city. The rich agricultural area around it, along with textile and leather industries within it, made its populous prosperous.

The letter makes reference to "an open door" (Rev. 3:8) which is set before the people by the authority of Christ Jesus Himself. Two interpretations of this "open door" are possible. First, it may be the door to the eternal kingdom. Not only can Jesus open the door to that opportunity, He *is* the Door (John 10:7, 9).

Compare "the key of David" with the "keys of death and of Hades" and the "keys of the kingdom":

Is. 22:22

Matt. 16:19

Rev. 1:18

Second, it may be the "door" of witness, service, and evangelistic opportunity. Philadelphia was described as the "gateway to the East." King Attalus II, the founder of the city, planned that it should be a center from which Greek culture might be propagated. This detail may explain the imagery here. Paul used the term in this way in 1 Corinthians 16:9 and 2 Corinthians 2:12.

Revelation 3:8 says the church had "little strength." When we are weak, we must depend on the Lord. The temptation will be to deny, to distort, or dilute God's Word to accommodate our weakness or vulnerability. But Jesus said they had shown biblical fidelity and had "kept My word, and not denied My name."

PROBING THE DEPTHS

Revelation 3:10 promises that Christ will keep believers "from the hour of trial," a promise whose specific reference has been debated by sincere Christian scholars and theologians. Regarding the timing of the rapture of the church, does this promise mean that believers will *escape from* the "trials" of the tribulation period, or that they will *endure through* the midst of them? Or, does "hour of trial" refer to that which was to come upon the Philadelphian church only?

The Greek phrase "keep from" (*tereo ek*) is used elsewhere only in John 17:15, where Christ prayed to the Father that He would "keep" believers from Satan.

Does He mean to preserve them from attack by the Evil One, or preserve them *through* such attack? Explain your response.

What about the rest of verse 10? Does the promise apply to the entire seven-year period (Daniel's Seventieth Week) or to the last three and one-half years (the "Great Tribulation"), when the "hour of temptation" comes to the "whole world"? Explain your choice.

God's only warning or directive to the Philadelphian congregation was ". . . hold fast what you have that no one may take your crown" (Rev. 3:11). God has gifted us with different skills, abilities, and gifts (1 Pet. 4:10, 11). Like the men in the parable of the talents, we need to use what we have, or else it will be taken away from us and given to another. Use the opportunities ("open doors") you have for God. He will commend and award you for it.

LAODICEA: THE LUKEWARM CHURCH
REVELATION 3:14–22

The city of Laodicea, forty-five miles southeast of Philadelphia, was a fortified city, and was named by Antiochus II, the

Greek king of Syria, who constructed it in the middle of the third century B.C. in honor of his wife, Queen Laodicea.

Situated in a volcanic region, the city was destroyed by an earthquake in A.D. 61. It was rebuilt by the efforts of its wealthy citizens without the aid of Nero, the Caesar. Thus, the whole community had a sense of pride and self-sufficiency.

In contrast to our Lord's letters to the other churches, where He conditioned His criticisms by first complimenting them, here at Laodicea He can find nothing good to say. He apparently had more respect for fiery hot fanaticism or icy cold formalism than for lifeless and lame lukewarmness (Rev. 3:17b). The church congregation at Laodicea was lukewarm and self-satisfied.

Even more pathetic, the Laodicean congregation were blind to their own spiritual lethargy. They measured their spiritual state or condition by their material wealth, thinking of themselves as "having it made." "You say, 'I am rich, have become wealthy, and have need of nothing'—and do not know that you are wretched, miserable, poor, blind, and naked" (Rev. 3:17). Whatever their relative wealth, they were not rich toward God.

They were trusting the signs of materialism as indicators of their spirituality. Read the story of the rich man in Luke 12:13–21. Why did God call him a "fool"?

Some people may be gifted by God with the ability to become wealthy. Read 1 Timothy 6:17–19 and list three things Paul instructs the rich people of the world to do with their money.

1.

2.

3.

Laodicea was noted for the preparation of a special salve which was said to be highly effective in the treatment of various ophthalmic disorders. Some of these believers had helped others to see physically, but they were blind spiritually. They could not see their own spiritual poverty nor the fact they had closed Christ out of their lives.

The letter concludes depicting a closed door of spiritual opportunity. Have you had times when you felt indifferent to God, or His work in the world?

What are the conditions of Christ's invitation in verse 20?

Do you sense any area where you may have shut Christ out of your life?

If your answer to either of the above questions was "yes," then Christ calls you to "be zealous and repent" (Rev. 3:19). He has promised to return and have fellowship with all who will open to Him.

 BIBLE EXTRA: REVELATION 3:20

This familiar passage and image of Christ standing outside a closed door awaiting invitation for entrance are not so much an appeal to sinners as they are to self-satisfied saints who have not allowed Christ sovereign control over their lives. The previous letter referred to an open door of opportunity (Rev. 3:8); now this letter depicts a closed door of spirituality. But the Savior is waiting to be invited in. Those who receive Him will enjoy once again His presence, His power, and His purpose.

In each of His letters to the seven churches, the Lord explicitly exhorts believers to be overcomers. What does He promise those who overcome the temptations and trials of this world? (Rev. 3:21)

How is this different from the position we have with Him now, "seated . . . in heavenly places"? (See Eph. 2:6–7.)

1. *Spirit-Filled Life Bible* (Nashville, TN: Thomas Nelson Publishers, 1991), 1954.
2. Ibid., 1960, "Word Wealth: Rev. 1:5, witness."
3. Ibid., "Kingdom Dynamics: Revelation 1:5, 6, Worship and Praise."
4. Ibid., note on Revelation 1:9.
5. Ibid., note on Revelation 1:10.
6. *Nelson's Quick-Reference Bible Maps and Charts* (Nashville, TN: Thomas Nelson Publishers, 1994), 324.
7. W. E. Vine, *An Expository Dictionary of Biblical Words* (Nashville, TN: Thomas Nelson Publishers), 414.
8. *Spirit-Filled Life Bible*, 1961.
9. "New Testament Heretics," *The Bible Almanac*, J. Packer, M. Tenney, W. White, Eds.; (Nashville, TN: Thomas Nelson Publishers, 1980), 537.
10. Jack W. Hayford with Gary Curtis, *Pathways to Pure Power (1 Corinthians)* (Nashville, TN: Thomas Nelson Publishers, 1994), 77.

Lesson 8/The Seven Seals
Revelation 4:1—8:1

In this section, we study the third and fourth divisions of John's Revelation: the *songs* of preparation, and the *seals* of judgment. Revelation 4 and 5 describe the awesome events the apostle saw concerning "things which must take place" in human history on earth prior to the judgments which are designed to deliver the planet from the control of the devil. John's heart was prepared for the pictures of fearful judgments by first seeing a vision of God's glory and triumph. It is important to perceive a principle here: all judgment is preceded by worship.

 WORD WEALTH

Worship, *proskuneo* (pros-koo-*neh*-oh); *Strong's #4352:* From *pros,* "toward," and *kuneo,* "to kiss." To prostrate oneself, bow down, do obeisance, show reverence, do homage, worship, adore. In the New Testament the word especially denotes homage rendered to God and the ascended Christ. All believers have a one-dimensional worship, to the only Lord and Savior. We do not worship angels, saints, shrines, relics, or religious personages.[1]

Based upon your reading of Revelation 4 and 5, do you believe John related the events in the sequential order they will take place on earth, or merely in the sequence of his receiving them?

Why would this matter?

BEHIND THE SCENES

Many students of prophetic study understand the apostle John to be primarily following a method known as *discursive description* in trying to communicate his vision. He seems to be relating the big picture of what he saw, digressing from one topic to another, without any particular regard for arranging his presentation by a simple sequence of time. For instance, the seven seals seem to be overlapping and integrated judgments continuing throughout human history.

THE THRONE ROOM OF HEAVEN
REVELATION 4:1–11

This passage offers the most complete picture of the throne of God in the Bible. Other glimpses are given in Ezekiel 1, Isaiah 6, and Psalms 18 and 82; but here is a scene integrating the majesty of the Almighty, the court of His cherubim and elders, and the Lion/Lamb Redeemer.

Who extends the invitation to "Come up here"? Compare Revelation 4:1 with 1:10.

What does this section tell us about the throne of God?

What did the four living creatures have in common? (Rev. 4:8)

How do they compare with the cherubim in Ezekiel 1 and 10?

What do these creatures do in other parts of the Revelation? (See Rev. 6:1–8; 15:7.)

About which of God's attributes do they speak and sing? (Rev. 6:8, 11)

Who are the "elders" of Revelation 6:4, 10 and 11, and what do they represent? Why are there twenty-four?

What might the phrase "sits on the throne" (Rev. 6:10) suggest about God's work?

 PROBING THE DEPTHS

INTERPRETIVE APPROACHES TO THE BOOK OF REVELATION
"Many devoted Christians are surprised to discover that other equally dedicated believers view the prophecies of the Book of Revelation differently from them. The book tolerates a wide spectrum of approaches, but the common denominator of all is the ultimate triumph of Jesus Christ, who culminates history with His final coming and reigns with and through His church forever.

The most popularized and widely discussed approach is called the *Dispensationalist* interpretation. This proposes that the Rapture of the church is referred to in Revelation 4:1, at which time the redeemed in Christ are translated into heaven at His coming 'in the air' (1 Thess. 4:17). Revelation 6—18 are perceived as the Great Tribulation (Matt. 24:21) or the wrath of God (1 Thess. 5:9) from which believers are kept (Rev. 3:10). This approach sees national Israel as God's people on Earth at this time (the church having been raptured), restored to Jerusalem, protected by *divine* seal (Rev. 7:1–8), worshiping in a rebuilt temple (Rev. 11:1–3), and suffering at the hand of the Antichrist.

Not as widely published but at least equally widely believed is the *Moderate Futurist* view. This proposes the Book of Revelation as summarizing the conclusion of the church's age-long procession through tribulation and triumph, warfare, and victory, and consummating in the climactic return of Jesus Christ for His church. The tribulation is generally viewed as age-long, but increasing in intensity, so that the church is understood as present through much of earth's turmoil until just prior to the outpouring of the 'bowls full of the wrath of God' (Rev. 15:7). This occurs during Revelation 16 and culminates in the collapse of the present world order (Rev. 17; 18).

Among other views are these: (1) The *Historic* position sees Revelation as a symbolic prophecy of the whole of church history, with the events of the book a picture of the events and movements that have shaped the conflict and progress of the Christian church. (2) The *Preterist* views Revelation as a message of hope and comfort to first-century believers only, offering them an expectation of their deliverance from Roman persecution and oppression. (3) The *Idealist* formulates no particular historical focus or effort at interpreting specifics of the book, rather seeing it as a broad, poetic portrayal of the conflict between the kingdom of God and the powers of Satan."[2]

Those who hold to the Futurist interpretation of prophecy believe the church is raptured between Revelation 3 and 4, though this event is not reported in the text. They argue from the absence of the church in the contextual details of Revelation 4—18. The fact that there is a trumpet sound and an invitation to John to "Come up here" is suggested as a type of the Rapture of the church prior to the Great Tribulation. Futurists note that the church reappears in Revelation 19—after the judgments—where she is seen in heaven and her marriage to the Lamb is announced (Rev. 19:7–9).

Other systems of interpretation suggest alternate views of the timing of the Rapture. Revelation 6:17, 7:9–17, 11:11–14, 14:14–16, and 19:14 will be studied as possible points of fulfillment of that heavenly promise.

THE LAMB TAKES THE SCROLL
REVELATION 5:1–7

In this setting, God is holding a book or scroll in His right hand. It is sealed with seven seals, which represent and reveal the pending judgments which are to try those who live on the earth.

Some have likened this sealed scroll to a title deed to a piece of property which is about to be redeemed by a relative. The judgments are what is required to drive out the enemy who is in unlawful possession of it.

When Adam sinned he lost his inheritance of the earth (Gen. 1:26–28), and it passed out of his hands into the possession of Satan, and resulted in the disinheritance of all of Adam's seed. The forfeited title deed is now in God's hands and is awaiting ultimate redemption by a "kinsman-redeemer." (See Lev. 25:23–28 and compare with Jer. 32:6–15.)

Since man forfeited his rule of this planet under God (Ps. 115:16), the earth has been in the grip of Satan (1 John 5:19). What biblical names for Satan substantiate this?

John 14:30

2 Cor. 4:4

What significance is it that the book is held in God's right hand?

Why is it the elder described a "Lion" as being worthy to open the book, but it was a wounded "Lamb" which did so?

What is suggested by the fact that the Lamb was slain, but is living? (See Is. 53 and John 1:29.)

When Jesus takes the book from His Father ("Him who sat on the throne"), He has the right to break its seals and claim the inheritance and dispossess the present claimant, Satan. This event is the fulfillment of Daniel's vision of the "Ancient of Days" in Daniel 7:9–14.

WORTHY IS THE LAMB
REVELATION 5:8–14

The four living creatures and the twenty-four elders are the first to worship the Lamb. They are followed in praise and worship by myriads of angels and all the redeemed humanity in heaven. Finally, every created being ("in heaven and on the earth and under the earth and such as are in the sea") joins the cosmic chorus. Their great theme, in answer to the earlier quest (Rev. 5:2, 3), is "Worthy is the Lamb."

Who sang a new song of redemption? (See Rev. 8:8–10)

What does John's vision say to us about the fulfillment of the Great Commission?

What four attributes did every created being ascribe to the Lamb?

1.

2.

3.

4.

What was the predetermined purpose of this cosmic chorus? (See Phil. 2:10, 11.)

Every created thing responds with honor, glory, and blessing to the Lord (Rev. 5:13). Worship is the means of fulfilling the purpose of our common creation.

The Lamb, invested with all the authority to execute judgment, begins now to open the first four seals with His nail-pierced hands. What we see in this ever-intensifying series of seal judgments is what our Lord called the "beginning of sorrows" (Matt. 24:8). This is thought by many to be the beginning of Daniel's Seventieth Week (Dan. 9:27).

FIRST SEAL: THE CONQUEROR
REVELATION 6:1, 2

When the Lamb broke the first seal, the first living creature cried with a voice of thunder, "Come and see." The cry is not addressed to John, but to one of the "Four Horsemen of the Apocalypse" on their errand of judgment.

List the important details of this first horseman:

Compare this rider with the white horse rider of Revelation 19:11–21.

BEHIND THE SCENES

The Dispensationalist would see this rider, who symbolized political conquest, as the Antichrist, who will come imitating Christ and claiming to be Him. (See Matt. 24:4, 5; John 5:43.)

Others would see this as descriptive of the delusion by which many antichrists have attempted to rule and deceive throughout church history (1 John 2:18). They understand Scripture to say that the visible church in a violent, unrepentant world will experience testing and tribulation along with the sinners. But God's sovereignty and promises provide a "sure and certain hope" for people of God's kingdom!

SECOND SEAL: CONFLICT ON EARTH
REVELATION 6:3, 4

The second living creature summoned the rider on a red horse, who was granted to "take peace from the earth."

What is stated about this rider to suggest or symbolize war?

THIRD SEAL: SCARCITY ON EARTH
REVELATION 6:5, 6

The inevitable result of worldwide anarchy and bloodshed is economic chaos. So the black horse rider, who appears at the breaking of the third seal, brings economic confusion on the earth.

What is the problem: famine, inflation, or scarcity of resources?

What is the scope of the problem's effects: luxuries, necessities, or . . . ?

FOURTH SEAL: WIDESPREAD DEATH ON EARTH
REVELATION 6:7, 8

The next rider is named "Death." And "Hades" (not "Hell"), that region of departed spirits, figuratively follows afterward to consume Death's victims.

Describe the extent of the destruction of human life at that time.

Compare this assault on human life and well-being with Jesus' predictions in Luke 21:11, 25.

FIFTH SEAL: THE CRY OF THE MARTYRS
REVELATION 6:9–11

When the fifth seal was peeled back, it revealed a completely different scene from those of the four horsemen. Now John sees under the altar in heaven the souls of them that had been slain "for the word of God and the testimony which they held." Perhaps these are the martyrs Jesus referred to in Matthew 24:9.

What did they call out? (Rev. 6:10)

What was given to them? What does this suggest about our resurrected bodies?

How long were they to wait?

Sixth Seal: Cosmic Disturbances
Revelation 6:12–17

The terrible cosmic catastrophes which are predicted to occur in connection with the breaking of the sixth seal are almost inconceivable. The language is typically apocalyptic and symbolic. Yet, these events were predicted elsewhere as the beginning of the wrath of God.

 Probing the Depths

"There are three basic streams of judgment issuing from the throne, summarized in the sets of seven seals, seven trumpets, and seven vials (bowls). These judgments are not necessarily successive in occurrence, but seem to overlap, interweave, and finally culminate together. (Note that each set, in culminating, involves a great earthquake [Rev. 6:12; 11:13; 16:18], suggesting they deal with different time spans and/or arenas of divine judgment, but that they climax simultaneously.)"[3]

Compare the sixth seal with the predictions of Isaiah 34:4; Joel 2:30, 31 and Matthew 24:29.

List the various startling physical changes that will cause a great fear to fall upon all classes and conditions of men.

Revelation 6:12 is kind of a pivot point in the otherwise age-long repetition of tribulation which Jesus predicted will occur when God expels evil from the earth. Men are finally going to see the seriousness of their circumstances, yet be unrepentant (Rev. 6:16).

BIBLE EXTRA

"Although the term 'The Rapture' is not in the Bible, the idea it represents is clearly present. By 'The Rapture' we refer to the literal, imminent (any moment) appearing of Jesus Christ from heaven, to take His redeemed church—the 'translated' living and the resurrected dead—to be with Him." [4]

Since God has not appointed His church to wrath (1 Thess. 5:19), what does the fact that "His wrath has come" in Revelation 6:17 suggest about the timing of the promised deliverance?

THE SEALING OF 144,000
REVELATION 7:1–8

It seems that times of tribulation give opportunity and motivation for witnessing. In Revelation 7, during an interlude in the dramatic descriptions of prophetic events, John sees two groups of people who will be especially used by God in grace during this period.

First are the 144,000 who will be "sealed" by God and protected from His wrath which is to come on the earth as judgment. Compare and contrast this "sealing" with those who will bear "the mark of the beast" in Revelation 13.

PROBING THE DEPTHS

"Three different views exist as to who the 144,000 may be.

The first is that they are a select group of Jewish converts to the Messiah who, in the wake of 'Tribulation' judgments (seven-year concept), turn to Jesus as Lord. They are then 'sealed' to preach the gospel to the world during this period after the church has been raptured.

The second is that they are a symbolic representation of the whole Church, including Jews and Gentiles (Rom. 2:28, 29); a preserved people kept throughout the age long era of the tribulation (classical concept) as witnesses to Christ.

The third is that they represent the full measure of God's fulfilling His commitment to His chosen people, the Jews. The Word of God clearly states that He has not left Israel derelict from His purposes (Rom. 9—11). Though they were 'broken off' (Rom. 11:17), there shall come a 'resurrection' of His purposed will for national Israel (Rom. 11:18) and a full complement of Jews shall be among the redeemed of all nations (Rom. 11:26)."[5]

TRIBULATION BELIEVERS
REVELATION 7:9–17

A second group of people to be uniquely used by God will be a mixed multitude of Gentiles (Rev. 7:9–17). This great group is international in scope (Rev. 7:9) composed of many ethnic and geographic groups who are either saved during these difficult days, or, if they may represent the larger group of redeemed saints, throughout all history.

In Revelation 7:11, 12, God is worshiped by an especially lovely list of terms. Write below the seven elements of adoration which are ascribed to God "forever and ever. Amen."

1.   5.

2.   6.

3.   7.

4.

This great multitude—which suddenly appears in heaven with white robes and palm branches—are so many that no one can number them. John has to ask who they are and where they came from (Rev. 7:13).

Write out the elder's response in Revelation 7:14:

Many would understand the elder's response (v. 14) to indicate that this great multitude represents the true church which has been raptured and caught up to the throne of heaven before the great Day of the Lord (God's wrath) begins.

BIBLE EXTRA

In Revelation 7:14 several terms need elaboration for better interpretation. For instance, *the ones who come out of;* literally, "ones coming out," a present participle, expressing a continuous and repeated action, not a once-for-all action. The action suggested harmonies with the general tribulation that takes place throughout the entire church age (see Rev. 1:9; Rev. 2:9, Rev. 22; Matt. 13:21; John 16:33; Acts 14:22; Rom. 8:35, 36; 12:12). The Great Tribulation, however, describes the acceleration and intensification of troublesome times as the Age comes to an end, climaxing with the Rapture and Second Coming.[6]

SEVENTH SEAL: PRELUDE TO THE SEVEN TRUMPETS
REVELATION 8:1

After the long interlude of Revelation 7, the final seal is broken. This seventh seal released a second series of judgments: the seven trumpet judgments, which deluge a doomed planet with destructive demonic activity.

What unique happening did John notice after the seventh seal was open?

This was a lull before the storm, as all heaven anticipated the final fulfillment of God's purposes. The Day of the Lord had come!

FAITH ALIVE

"The significance of this entire analysis is that it demonstrates the mighty fact that God's progressive pattern of advancing the judgments which finally expel all evil from the earth are directly related to the praise, the worship, and the prayers of His people. There may be no mightier statement in all the Bible on the truth of "Kingdom entry through worship" than that revealed in this Book. It is *present praise* that gives room for His presence and power among His people (Ps. 22:3); and as shown in Revelation, it is *age-long worship* which releases His ultimate entry and dominion—the Forever Kingdom of our Lord (Rev. 19:1–7)."[7]

How is your "praise-life"? Our study in Revelation has revealed that present praise and accumulated adoration releases God's kingdom purposes. Rate yourself on a scale of 1–10 as a "present praiser."

1	2	3	4	5	6	7	8	9	10
Puny Praiser					Periodic Praiser			Present, Persistent Praiser	

Re-read Revelation 4 and 5 and then write a paragraph of praise to God for who He is.

Review Revelation 7:9–12. Which aspects of adoration seem unclear to you?

1. *Spirit-Filled Life Bible,* (Nashville, TN: Thomas Nelson Publishers, 1991), 1967, "Word Wealth: Rev. 4:10 worship."

2. Ibid., 1966, "Kingdom Dynamics, Revelation 4:1, Interpretive Approaches to the Book of Revelation."

3. Jack W. Hayford, "A Survey of the Book of Revelation" (Van Nuys, CA: Living Way Ministries, 1985), 3.

4. Jack W. Hayford, "Unlocking Revelation Study Notes" (Van Nuys, CA: Living Way Ministries, 1991), 7.

5. Ibid., 6.

6. *Spirit-Filled Life Bible,* 1971, note on Revelation 7:14.

7. Jack W. Hayford, "A Survey of the Book of Revelation," 3.

Lesson 9/The Seven Trumpets
Revelation 8:2—11:18

It would seem that the seventh seal actually contains the seven trumpet judgments which call the waiting world to repentance. They differ from what preceded or follows.

- The seals reveal the *comprehensive* judgments released by God;
- the trumpets reveal the *controlling* judgments, the extent of which are restricted by God; and
- the vials reveal the *climaxing* judgments, which are poured out rapidly by the wrath of God.[1]

Worship and intercession appear to be the two spiritual forces which release the seven trumpet judgments (Rev. 8:1–5). In response to "the prayers of all the saints" (Rev. 8:3), God allows demonic forces to impact the world around and within. "The first four trumpets are similar to some of the plagues in Egypt (Exodus 7—10) and relate essentially to environmental and ecological pollution and/or deterioration. The last three create psychological torment (Rev. 9:5, 6) and convey physical destruction (Rev. 9:18)."[2]

FIRST TRUMPET: VEGETATION STRUCK
REVELATION 8:7

What are we told will rain from heaven in judgment?

How much damage will be inflicted?

Second Trumpet: The Seas Struck
Revelation 8:8, 9

What will be cast into the sea? (Rev. 8:8)

What might this action (if symbolic) represent?

How much damage is done?

Third Trumpet: The Waters Struck
Revelation 8:10–13

How is this judgment described?

What do you think it means?

Could it be the results of fallout radiation from a nuclear explosion?

What is the name of the star?

How has God used wormwood in the past? (See Lam. 3:15; Jer. 9:13–15; and 23:15.)

Fourth Trumpet: The Heavens Struck
Revelation 8:12, 13

Could this darkness result from the light-reducing blanket of smoke produced by the three previous trumpet judgments?

What is the significance of the repeated "woes" in verse 13?

Fifth Trumpet: The Locust from the Bottomless Pit
Revelation 9:1–12

Up to this point mankind has not been touched directly by these trumpet judgments. However, the next two plagues are on people themselves, and John gives more than twice the space to their description than the previous four trumpets together.

The account begins with a *star* falling from heaven to the earth (Rev. 9:1). The personal pronouns and personal acts ascribed to this star indicate this is more than a meteor.

What is this fallen star given in verse one?

What did the "star" do with it?

What happened when the "bottomless pit" is opened by this fallen star? (Rev. 9:2, 3)

What are the Hebrew and Greek names given in Revelation 9:11 for this "angel of the bottomless pit," which is also king of the locust-like creatures?

✍️	**WORD WEALTH**

Abaddon means "destruction" (see Job 26:6), which in Greek is *Apollyon,* which means "exterminator" or "destroyer" (see 1 Cor. 10:10). These are names for Satan, himself a fallen angel (see Revelation 12:7–12; Is. 14:12–14; Ezek 28:11–17).

The Locust-scorpion-horse creatures with humanlike faces and hair symbolize demonic beings (see Ex. 10:12–15; Joel 1:1—2:11). Rather than stripping the vegetation, these creatures attack and torment only certain human beings for a period of five months.

Who are these selected victims?

Some have tried to explain the creatures in this vision as helicopters with chemical sprays. Others have suggested the creatures to be "killer bees." What do you think? Why?

God has set a "restraining" force in the world to hold back the full effects of wickedness (2 Thess. 2:6, 7). At some point in this terrible Tribulation, God will remove this gracious ministry and the demonic deluge will follow unrestrained.

SIXTH TRUMPET: THE ANGELS FROM THE EUPHRATES REVELATION 9:13–21

This judgment is so severe that "a third of mankind" will be killed by four extremely wicked and powerful angels who had been bound and reserved for this great day of judgment. (See Jude 6.) They are loosed at God's command.

How many million were drawn together in an army to accomplish this terrible task?

What kind of army is meant—a literal human army, an army of demons, or . . . ?

If a literal human army is intended, consider the logistical challenge there would be to raise, arm, and transport a human army to destroy *one third of mankind*!

What was the purpose of the plagues resulting from the effects of war?

How does the massive destruction by fire relate to Peter's understanding of the events of the last days? (See 2 Pet. 3:7–9.)

THE MIGHTY ANGEL WITH THE LITTLE BOOK
REVELATION 10:1–11

Before the seventh and last trumpet is sounded, there are some significant things discussed during a second interlude. This period follows the same pattern as in the seals, where additional information prepares the reader for the developments to follow.

The apostle saw a mighty angel (possibly Michael, "the great prince" [Dan. 12:1]). Summarize the dazzling description of this angel (vv. 1–6):

In his hand the angel had a small scroll (Rev. 10:2). It is different from the scroll of Revelation 5—7. It might be connected with the symbolic scroll of Ezekiel (Ezek. 2:9—3:3; see also Jer. 15:15–17).
What is the prophet told to do with the scroll?

Notice that John is likewise told to eat the scroll when it was given to him (Rev. 10:9, 10). This action symbolizes assimilating the Word of God into our being so it can be obeyed and proclaimed with confidence.

BIBLE EXTRA

The immense angelic figure is said to have one foot on the sea and the other on the land. This symbolizes that the prophetic message is for the whole world. His message, which sounded to John like loud claps of thunder, was understood by John, but he was instructed not to write it down, but rather to seal it up.

Other things have been kept, unrevealed to mankind for the time being. Discover these in the following passages:

Dan. 8:26

Dan. 12: 4, 9

2 Cor. 12:4

As the angel holds the scroll in his left hand, he lifts his right hand to heaven and underscores the importance of this long-awaited announcement by swearing to its truth. This action is similar to when a witness is sworn into court and takes an oath to tell the truth.

What is the message and its meaning? (Rev. 10:6)

What mystery will be revealed or completed? (Rev. 10:7) (See 1 Cor. 15:50–52.)

As mentioned earlier, eating the book has to do with the assimilation of the message it contains. The content of the message John is to "eat" is uncertain, but the effect on John is both bitter and sweet. The judgments are sweet because they bring a proper end to evil. On the other hand, they are also bitter because proclaiming the wrath of God on unrepentant recipients is an unpleasant experience.

THE TWO WITNESSES
REVELATION 11:1–14

In John's continuing vision he was given a "reed" to use as a measuring rod to "measure the temple of God, the altar, and those who worship there."

 ### BEHIND THE SCENES

This Tribulation period temple is the fourth temple mentioned in the Scriptures. The first temple, built by Solomon, was destroyed in 586 B.C. by Nebuchadnezzar. Antiochus Epiphanes, in 168 B.C., desecrated and destroyed the second temple which was (re)built by Ezra and Nehemiah after the Exile. The third temple, which Herod completed in Jesus' day, was destroyed in A.D. 70 by Titus Vespasian. This fourth temple, which is the focus of attention during the Great Tribulation period, will be followed by a fifth temple during the Millennium (Ezek. 40—47).

The actual edifice John is to measure is called a *naos* in Greek. This word means a "shrine or central sanctuary." It is like the sacred areas of the Holy Place and the Most Holy Place (NKJV) in the previous temples of Jerusalem, into which only the priests could lawfully enter. It is mentioned in 2 Thessalonians 2:4 as the seat of the Man of Sin.

So the temple spoken of in Revelation 3:12; 7:15; 11:19; 14:15, 17; 15:5, 6, 8; and 16:1, 17 *could* be some structure other than a rebuilt temple occupying the same space as the current Moslem "Dome of the Rock" on the Temple Mount. We can be sure it is a place of worship, someplace in Jerusalem, during this period of Tribulation.

In measuring the "temple," John was instructed not to measure part of it. What was that section and the reason for skipping it? (v. 2)

How long is this outer court to be trampled underfoot?

How does this correspond to Daniel's Seventieth Week? (cf. Dan 9:24–27)

If the months are typical "prophetic months" of thirty days each, how does this time frame correlate with the time which is given to the two witnesses to speak for God on earth?

 ## PROBING THE DEPTHS

Though the "two witnesses" are not identified as individuals, they are reminiscent of Moses and Elijah as well as of Enoch and Elijah. One of Moses' greatest miracles was the turning of water into blood, and one of Elijah's was shutting up the sky. However, man is said to die only once, and Moses has died and is still buried on Mount Nebo in Jordan. Enoch and Elijah are the only two men who have been taken by the Lord directly without dying (see Malachi 4:5, 6 and Mark 9:11–13).

Further speculation abounds as to the identities of the two central persons. One is that the "two witnesses" are actually two "companies" of appointed witnesses of God who are empowered in a special way during this time. Finally, some have suggested since the opening two verses are clearly spiritual and symbolic, that there is no reason to make the rest of the passage anything else than the same.[3]

These two witnesses—whoever they may be—will be supernaturally protected and given special anointed words to speak and special powers over nature (Rev. 11:5, 6). The precision of the length of their ministry suggests strongly for one-half of the Seventieth Week of Daniel—probably the latter.

What happens when the two witnesses are attacked? (See Rev. 11:5, and 2 Kings 1:9–15.)

What must happen before the witnesses can be overcome by the beast from the bottomless pit? (See Rev. 11:7.)

How will the inhabitants of Jerusalem, "where also our Lord was crucified," respond to their deaths? (Rev. 11:8–10)

How is it possible for the entire world to view the bodies of the two witnesses at the same time? (Rev. 11:9)

After three and a half days, the two witnesses are resurrected by "the breath of life from God." How did the rejoicing people react?

In Revelation 11:12, a voice from heaven speaks to the res-urrected witnesses and calls them to " 'Come up here.' And they ascended to heaven in a cloud."

PROBING THE DEPTHS

Some people would say verse 12 describes the Rapture (1 Thess. 4:16, 17) and is symbolic of all the Christians going up into heaven. If so, then the Rapture occurs
- at the end of the second half of Daniel's Seventieth Week,
- at the end of the Great Tribulation, and
- after the persecution of the Antichrist.

Some who hold to this time period for the Rapture see a similarity with the "clouds" which receive the two witnesses and the "clouds" in which both living and dead believers will be caught up at the Lord's return (Matt. 24:29, 30; 1 Thess. 4:15–18).

We cannot be dogmatic as to when the Rapture of the church will occur, but we can be assured that it will!

AT A GLANCE

RAPTURE EVENT	Matt. 24	1 Cor. 15	1 Thess. 4	Rev. 11
Lord in the air	X		X	
Shout			X	X
Trumpet		X	X	X
Dead in Christ raised	X	X	X	X
Living believers caught up*	X	X	X	X

*"caught up" (Gr., *harpadzo*): to seize, snatch away, catch up, be taken suddenly by force.

What natural disaster occurs in Jerusalem at the time of the resurrection and ascension of the two witnesses? (See Rev. 11:13.)

What were the results and responses?

THE SEVENTH TRUMPET: THE KINGDOM PROCLAIMED
REVELATION 11:15–18

As the seventh angel sounds the seventh (and last) trumpet, the final triumph of God and Christ is proclaimed in terms of the reign of King Jesus over the earth and all eternity. There is a transference of power and authority to the rightful Owner and true King: "The kingdoms of this world have become the kingdoms of our Lord and of His Christ, and He shall reign forever and ever!" (Rev. 11:15).

BIBLE EXTRA

"God made known to Paul that the dead will be raised up by instantaneous transformation **at the last trumpet.** Trumpets were used to call God's people together (Num. 10:1–10) and at royal coronations in presenting kings to Israel (1 Kin. 1:34). The Rapture of the church not only transforms us but welcomes Christ the coming King on Earth, as we 'meet the Lord in the air' at His returning (see 1 Thess. 4:16, 17)."[4]

The recitation of the twenty-four elders (Rev. 11:17, 18) is a synopsis of the remaining chapters of Revelation. It previews the dreadful vial/bowl judgments which follow.

PROBING THE DEPTHS

"The bursting of the amniotic sack, during natural childbirth, generally testifies that the dilation stage has been completed and the expulsion phase has begun. Likewise, the seventh trumpet will announce the expulsion of the two seeds. First, it will proclaim the completion of the church, initiating its harvest from the earth and, thereby, bringing the servants of all ages into the presence of God to receive their just rewards

(Rev. 11:15–18). Second, it will announce the collapse of sin's dominion in the earth. This will initiate the gathering of the tares of all nations to Armageddon to resist the coming of the Lord, and will usher in the wrath of God."[5]

The readers of the Old Testament prophets (as well as Paul's epistles) had to understand the matter of "the last trump" without any knowledge of the Book of Revelation. What connection would they have made between the Day of the Lord and the blowing of a trumpet?

Joel 2:1

Zeph. 1:14–16

1 Cor. 15:51, 52

1 Thess. 4:16, 17

 FAITH ALIVE

Re-read Revelation 11:17 and make it your prayer too:

"We give thanks, O Lord God Almighty,
The One who is and who was and who is to come,
Because You have taken Your great power and reigned!"

1. Jack W. Hayford, "A Survey of the Book of Revelation" (Van Nuys, CA: Living Way Ministries, 1985), 4.

2. Ibid., 5.

3. Ibid., 6.

4. *Spirit-Filled Life Bible* (Nashville, TN: Thomas Nelson Publishers, 1991), 1745, note on 1 Corinthians 15:51, 52.

5. John L. Dudley, *The Harvest* (Peterborough, NH: Inspirational Publishing Co., 1984), 66, 67. Jack W. Hayford, "Unlocking Revelation: The Heavenly Temple" (Van Nuys, CA: Living Way Ministries), 15.

Lesson 10/The Seven Signs
Revelation 11:19—15:4

In this section, the scene turns from the effects of the seventh trumpet on earth, to the events occurring simultaneously in heaven and in the heavenlies. Specific physical and political events are symbolically pictured.

Revelation 11 ends with a picture of heaven opening to receive God's kingdom which was on earth. In verse 19 we see into the temple in heaven—of which the earthly tabernacle and temples were but a type or copy (see Heb. 9:23–26). "The throne is the ark of His covenant, specifically the Mercy Seat (see Ex. 25:8, 9, 10–22; Heb. 9:23–26), a reminder of God's faithfulness in remembering His people."[1]

THE WOMAN, THE CHILD, AND THE DRAGON
REVELATION 12:1–6

Up until this point, most of the Book of Revelation has concerned God's glory and His judgments against unbelievers on earth. Now, in the interlude indicated in Revelation 10—15, the drama shifts to seven *signs* (miniature vignettes) symbolically portraying portions of the Tribulation, not necessarily in chronological order.

The first scene presents an allegory with which the ancient world would have been familiar. A usurper plots to succeed to the throne by killing the royal child-prince at birth. The prince is miraculously rescued and hidden away until he is old enough to kill the usurper and claim his kingdom.

What are the names used for the "usurper" in this passage? (See Rev. 12:3, 9; Is. 27:1.)

How do the seven diadems identify him with the last of the Gentile rulers of Daniel's dreams? (See Dan. 7:7, 8 and Revelation 13:1–7.)

Who might be represented by "a third of the stars of heaven"? (See Rev. 12:7; Matt. 25:41; Eph. 6:12.)

Who is the pregnant woman? (See Gen. 37:9, 10; Is. 26:17, 18; 66:7ff.; Mic. 4:10; 5:3.)

Who is the Man-Child? (See v. 5, Ps. 2:7–9; Dan. 7:13; and Acts 1:9.)

What was the reason the dragon persecuted the woman? (See Rev. 12:13.)

Where does the woman flee for protection? (See Rev. 12:6, 14; Isa. 16:1–5; Dan. 11:36–45; Hos. 2:14–23.)

SATAN THROWN OUT OF HEAVEN
REVELATION 12:7–12

The second vignette depicts the same spiritual conflict as shown above (Rev. 12:1–6), but now it is described from the heavenly realm.

Who is "Michael" and against whom does he fight in Revelation 12:7–9? (See Dan. 10:13, 21; 12:1; Jude 9.)

 BEHIND THE SCENES

In another important prophetic passage (2 Thess. 2:1–9), the Apostle Paul describes the sequence of events which leads to the clear understanding of exactly who the Antichrist really is. Before he can be revealed, "he who now restrains will do so until he is taken out of the way" (Rev. 12:7).

"The restrainer is mentioned nowhere else in the Bible. Among interpretations proposed for the restraining power that keeps the Antichrist in check have been (1) Paul's incomplete ministry: the son of perdition would emerge once Paul's mission is complete; (2) the Holy Spirit, who keeps things under control until the ripe eschatological moment; (3) God Himself, since it is evil that is held back; (4) the Jewish state at the time; and (5) the institution of human government."[2]

Still others have hinted at Michael, the archangel who is frequently implicated in end-time events. It is clear that Michael has been the appointed angelic guardian and champion of Israel (Dan. 10:13, 21; 12:1; Jude 9). It is also significant that he is specifically mentioned in the battle with Satan and his fallen angels before they are cast to the earth. If Michael no longer "stands up" for Israel (Dan. 12:1), then there is nothing to restrain Satan from the repulsive actions as "the man of sin" described in 2 Thess. 4:1–12 as a part of the great apostasy of the end times.

Satan is also identified as "that serpent of old" (Rev. 12:9). Some would see a connection with the serpent in the Garden of Eden (Gen. 3) as well as the Lord's promise to punish the ancient sea serpent called Leviathan (Is. 26:29—27:1). What do you think?

The familiar passage of 12:11 reminds us that the brethren overcame the enemy during this time of persecution by appropriating the victory of the finished work of the Cross ("the blood of the Lamb") and by the patient, public confession of their faith ("the word of their testimony"). They loved Jesus more than life itself ("they did not love their lives to the death")!

THE WOMAN PERSECUTED
REVELATION 12:13–17

What does the dragon do immediately after being cast down upon the earth?

Where was the woman taken for protection during this time?

Compare Revelation 12:6 with 12:14. If a prophetic month is thirty days, how many years is this? How is this period related in Revelation 12:14?

How does the Serpent attempt to attack the woman? How is she protected?

THE BEAST FROM THE SEA
REVELATION 13:1–10

This first half of chapter 13 describes a hideous beast coming out of the sea. This is the first of two beasts who will have great authority and power in the rest of Revelation. The first will have great political power and the second (13:11), significant religious support to influence the political aims of the first.

This first beast, which rises "up out of the sea," is usually understood as the Antichrist John mentions in his smaller epistle (1 John 2:18).

 BIBLE EXTRA

The biblical idea of the Antichrist is variously shown to be:
- A general spirit: (1 John 2:18, 22; 4:3; 2 John 7; Rev. 13:1, 2)
- The world's system: (Dan. 2:24, 25; 7:23–27)
- A human being: (Dan. 7:25; 8:22–26; 11:36–45; 2 Thess. 2:1–12)

Is the "sea" (Rev. 13:1) literally a body of water, or a symbolic representation of something else? (See Rev. 13:15.)

The monster's makeup reminds us of the beasts Daniel saw in his vision in Daniel 7:2–7. Why would John alter the order of the qualities of the beast compared to Daniel's description?

What three things did the Dragon (Satan) give John's sea beast?

The beast is "mortally wounded" in one of its seven heads (Rev. 13:3) by a military weapon (v. 14). Do you think this was inflicted on an individual emperor or an entire empire?

PROBING THE DEPTHS

A study of related passages (e.g., Dan. 7:23–27; 8:22–26; 11:36–45; Ezek. 38:2, 4, 8, 9; 2 Thess. 2:1–12; Rev. 13:3; 17:8–11) reveal to some students of eschatology that this final Antichrist is a man (possibly a Japhethite from the ancestral line of Magog) who was killed by a fatal wound to the head by a military weapon, and who will come back to life to rule the final beast empire of Satan. How would a seemingly miraculous recovery/resurrection from such a wound enhance the power and authority of this new world dictator and the dragon?

In Revelation 13:5–8, what four things are "given" to the beast, and by whom?

1.

2.

3.

4.

The period of the beast's authority is limited. Compare Revelation 13:5 with 11:2, 3 and 12:6, 14, along with Daniel 9:27 and 12:6, 7. Then write down the length of his dominion.

The Jews used lunar years to measure time. Consequently in the interpretation of biblical prophecies the application of the lunar year is generally accepted as a "prophetic year."

A lunar year is comprised of thirty-day months. Revelation 13:5–8 states that the Antichrist is empowered to blaspheme God and to make war with the saints for how many months? How many days would that be?

Five separate events occur during the reign of the Antichrist which are specifically stated as extending for either 1260 days, 42 months, or three and one-half years. Identify the period mentioned in each of the following scriptures:

Dan. 7:25

Rev. 11:2

Rev. 11:3

Rev. 12:6

Rev. 13:5–8

What is said in Revelation 13:7 to imply that there are believers on earth at this time?

The beast is given Messiah-like authority by the Dragon (Luke 4:4–7; 2 Thess. 2:4; 1 John 5:19). Who worships this false messiah? (See v. 8.)

THE BEAST FROM THE EARTH
REVELATION 13:11–18

Just as the first beast came up out of the sea (possibly the churning political chaos of modern governments), now John sees another beast coming up out of the earth. Whereas the dictator beast was symbolized by powerful animal images, this second beast is said to be like a lamb, but he spoke with the same authority as the Dragon.

How is this second beast identified in Revelation 16:13, 19:20, and 20:10?

What kind of miracles is this false prophet able to perform? (See Rev. 13:13–15.)

In an attempt to force people to worship the image of the beast (v. 15) the false prophet initiates a plan. What is the connection between economics and worship in this evil plan? (v. 17)

BEHIND THE SCENES

Since neither the Hebrew nor the Greek language possessed a separate numerical system, the letters of their alphabets carried numerical value. Hence, the symbolic **number of the beast** is the sum of the numerical values of the separate letters of his name. The monster may be the last of many pseudo-Messiahs (see Matt. 24:24; Mark 13:22) to arise in history who manifest the spirit of antichrist. See 1 John 2:18, 19, 22; 4:3; 2 John 7.[5]

THE LAMB AND THE 144,000
REVELATION 14:1–5

Do you feel the location of Revelation 14:1 is an actual geographical setting or a description of a spiritual reality? Why?

BEHIND THE SCENES

Zion was originally the name of the ancient Jebusite hillside fortress which David captured near the Kidron Valley. He called this stronghold of Zion "the City of David" (1 Kings 8:1; 1 Chron. 11:5; 2 Chron. 5:2). After Solomon built the temple on the adjacent Mount Moriah, the word Zion was expanded in meaning to include the entire temple area. Eventually Zion was used figuratively for all of Jerusalem, then for the land of Judah, and finally it came to mean the entire nation of Israel. The New Testament writer to the Hebrews gave it another meaning by relating it to "the city of the Living God, the heavenly Jerusalem" (Heb. 12:22).

What two names are written on the foreheads of the 144,000? Compare this with the requirements of Revelation 13:16–18. What is significant in this comparison?

The new song (Rev. 14:3) sung by the 144,000 is a song only the redeemed can understand and sing. How do Ephesians 5:19 and Colossians 3:16 enhance our "choir practice" before that performance?

THE PROCLAMATION OF THREE ANGELS
REVELATION 14:6–13

In this third scene we see three angels with three messages. The first angel (Rev. 14:6, 7) presents a call to "those who dwell on the earth—to every nation, tribe, tongue, and people" to honor the Creator, "who made heaven and earth, the sea and springs of water." This "messenger" was evangelizing in the midst of judgment. There is no mention of Jewish evangelists or Christian witnesses, yet the grace of God provides the preaching of "the everlasting gospel."

The second angel then flies with a declaration of doom. It announces the collapse of a great city. What city is mentioned? What do you know of that city today?

How influential was the fallen city?

The third angel warns of eternal judgment on those who are Beast-marked or worshippers of the Beast. Describe the nature and extent of their judgment:

All of these messages underscore the importance of patient endurance by the saints, who must "keep the commandments of God and the faith of Jesus." What ongoing fruitfulness is promised to the dead in Christ?

REAPING THE EARTH'S HARVEST
REVELATION 14:14–16

The harvest is used in the Old Testament for divine judgment (Hos. 6:11; Joel 3:13). Likewise, Jesus related the final judgment to the harvest of the earth (Matt. 13:30, 39).

Many identify this vision of a two-phased harvest as the final eschatological judgment. Some interpret the first phase as believers being "harvested" from the earth and into the Lord's presence before unbelievers are "gathered" like grapes for crushing. Others see this the second judgment as a restating of the first, emphasizing the kind and extent of judgment.

Who is identified in the cloud?

What is he instructed to do by "another angel"?

Who is the reaper?

What, in your view, is the harvest that is reaped?

REAPING THE GRAPES OF WRATH
REVELATION 14:17–20

"Another angel" came out of the temple in heaven, and with yet "another angel" initiated a great gathering of grapes. This second harvest is often suggested as the ultimate wrath of God which is to be poured out on the unbelieving earth-dwellers in the bowl/vial judgments which follow in Revelation 16.

How is this gathering different from the harvesting in Revelation 14:15, 16?

How severe is the violence and carnage of this second judgment? (Rev. 14:20)

Do you believe this gruesome account is literal or a literary hyperbole? Compare Revelation 14:20 with 16:13–16 and 19:11–21 before you answer.

PRELUDE TO THE BOWL JUDGMENTS
REVELATION 15:1–4

Revelation 15 concludes this celestial interlude which serves as a prelude to the last series of seven punitive plagues (Rev. 15:1) in Revelation. The plagues are preceded by various victorious saints singing special songs of praise for the redemption which is theirs.

What songs are specifically mentioned in Revelation 15:3?

What can be learned about God in the lyrics which are recorded in Revelation 15:3, 4?

 FAITH ALIVE

Majesty

Majesty, worship His Majesty.
  Unto Jesus be all glory, honor, and praise.
Majesty, kingdom authority flows from His throne unto His own;
  His anthem raise.
So exalt, lift up on high the name of Jesus.
  Magnify, come glorify Christ Jesus the King.
Majesty, worship His Majesty;
  Jesus who died, now glorified, King of all kings.[6]

How do the lyrics of the chorus "Majesty" express qualities of the "Lord God Almighty" similar to those in Revelation 15:3, 4? (Note: the composer uses the term "His Majesty" as a *title* for Christ, not as a description of His glory; thus, this call is not to worship a radiance or quality, but to worship the King Himself.)

We don't have to wait until we are standing before God's throne in heaven to magnify His Majesty. List three things about Jesus for which you would praise Him right now:

1.

2.

3.

1. *Spirit-Filled Life Bible* (Nashville, TN: Thomas Nelson Publishers, 1991), 1976, note on Revelation 11:19.

2. Ibid., 1836, note on 2 Thessalonians 2:6, 7.

3. Ibid., 1977–1978, "Kingdom Dynamics: Rev. 12:10, 11, New Testament: Age-long Warfare."

4. Ibid., 1994, "Truth-in-Action through Revelation: #2."

5. Ibid., 1980, note on Revelation 13:18.

6. Jack W. Hayford, "Majesty," © 1981, Rocksmith Music, ASCAP. All rights reserved. Used by permission.

Lesson 11/The Seven Bowls
Revelation 15:5—16:21

If the first phase of the final judgment (Rev. 14:14–16) represents believers being "harvested" from the earth and into the Lord's presence, then Revelation 15 can be thought of as a detailed account of what happens to them in heaven. Likewise, chapter 16 details what transpires in the second phase for those who have embraced evil on the earth.

From the heavenly counterpart of the earthly "tabernacle of testimony" (see Ex. 40:34, 35), seven angels, dressed as priests, came out to execute the wrath of God in the earth (Rev. 15:1, 5–7; 16:1).

  WORD WEALTH

Testimony, *marturion* (mar-*too*-ree-on); *Strong's #3142*: Compare "martyr" and "martyrology." Proof, evidence, witness, proclamation of personal experience. The tabernacle, which evidences God's presence, is a testimony to the covenant between Him and His people.[1]

Revelation 15:8 states that the temple in heaven "was filled with the smoke from the glory of God and from His power." Where else in Scripture do we read of "holy smoke" and the visible glory of God?

Compare the content of the following scriptures:

Ex. 40:34, 35

1 Kings 8:10, 11

Is. 6:1–4

What contains this final expression of the wrath of God? (See Rev. 15:1, 7, 8 and 16:1.)

Who instructs the seven angels to pour out the bowls? (16:1)

AT A GLANCE

THE SEVEN PLAGUES, REVELATION 16:
1. Horrible sores on the Beast-marked, v. 2
2. Sea polluted into total devastation, v. 3 (cf. 8:8, 9)
3. Waters turn to blood—pollution, vv. 4–7 (cf. 8:10, 11)
4. Sun scorches mankind, vv. 8, 9.
5. Darkness and pain on the power brokers, vv. 10, 11 (cf. 9:6)
6. The last surge of demonic furies, vv. 12–16 (cf. 9:13–15)
7. The final shaking of the Earth, vv. 17–21 (cf. 6:12–17; 11:15–19; Heb. 12:25–29).[2]

Demonic spirits, under the control of the "unholy trinity" (16:13) manipulate the kings of the earth to what event? (See 16:14, 16.)

Explain how Revelation 16:15 is both a hope-filled promise for the believer and a haunting prediction for the unbeliever.

This reference to "a thief in the night" (16:15) links together four other passages which refer the Lord's coming suddenly and unexpectedly in judgment. What can be learned from each about the believer's need for readiness?

• Luke 12:39, 40

• 2 Pet. 3:10

• Rev. 3:3

• Rev. 16:15

In Matthew 24:45–47 how does Christ suggest his followers should serve Him while His return is delayed?

THE SEVENTH BOWL: THE EARTH UTTERLY SHAKEN
REVELATION 16:17–21

The seventh plague is finally poured out by the seventh angel. It is not poured out on the earth, but rather "into the air." We are not told what this means. Some see significance in that this is said to be the abode of Satan, the "prince of the powers of the air" (Eph. 2:2). Others feel it indicates that this last judgment is universal.

What does the loud voice from the temple of heaven say?

Compare Revelation 15:1 and 15:8, and explain what this saying suggests.

What natural catastrophes are described in Revelation 16:18?

What geophysical terms are used to describe the devastating destruction? (Rev. 16:18–20)

BIBLE EXTRA

How heavy were the hailstones which fell from heaven? (Check study notes or margin references in your Bible [or under "weights and measurements" in a Bible dictionary] to determine the approximate weight of a "talent" in modern pounds.)

How is this similar to other instances in Scripture when God used hail as a weapon of destruction? (See Ex. 9:13–25 and Josh. 10:1.)

Just as the law of Israel required the stoning to death of the blasphemer (Lev. 24:16), so here the blasphemers of the end time shall be stoned to death from Heaven!

Revelation 16:19 says the "great city" is split into three parts and all the cities of the nations fall as well. In Revelation 11:8–13 a "great city" experienced an earthquake which killed 7,000 people. How do we know that city was (at least spiritually symbolic of) Jerusalem? (See Rev. 11:8.)

What other geophysical predictions can be found in Scripture about the city of Jerusalem?

Is. 2:2

Ezek. 40:2

Mic. 4:1

Zech. 14:10

However, in Revelation 17 and 18 we will see Babylon called "the great city." Perhaps the term symbolizes the seat of earthly empires, which falls in the most destructive earthquake ever experienced by mankind.

This final plague brings about horrific destruction amidst unparalleled convulsions of nature. How do the surviving people respond to God?

1. *Spirit-Filled Life Bible* (Nashville, TN: Thomas Nelson Publishers, 1991), 1982, "Word Wealth: Revelation 15:5, testimony."

2. Jack W. Hayford, "Unlocking Revelation Study Notes" (Van Nuys, CA: Living Way Ministries, 1991), 15.

Lesson 12/The Seven Spectacles
Revelation 17:1—20:3

Just as the unrepentant people of earth were judged because of their wickedness, the major perpetrators of evil will likewise meet their just rewards in God's prophetic timetable. With graphic detail, John relates dramatic displays of the demonic and Divine as God judges the Antichrist, False Prophet, and Satan, and the systems they controlled.

THE BEAUTY RIDES THE BEAST
REVELATION 17:1–18

When the great global earthquake of the last plague leveled the cities of the world, John called attention to one city in particular. Which was it? (Rev. 16:19)

In Revelation 17 and 18 John revisits that destruction and deals in detail with the fall of Babylon, which he calls "MYSTERY BABYLON THE GREAT" and "THE MOTHER OF HARLOTS" (Rev. 17:5). This reference seems to indicate she has daughters who are also "harlots." A harlot is a woman who fornicates for financial or commercial gain.

 WORD WEALTH

Committed Fornication, *porneuo* (porn-yoo-oh); *Strong's #4203:* Compare "pornographic" and "pornography." To engage in illicit sexual intercourse, be unfaithful, play the

harlot, prostitute oneself. The word is used literally (Mark 10:19;
1 Cor. 6:18; 10:8; Rev. 2:14, 20) and metaphorically to describe
spiritual fornication, that is, idolatry (Rev. 17:2; 18:3, 9).[1]

The influence and authority of the woman is indicated by
what terms? (See Rev. 17:1, 2, 15.)

In Rev. 17:3–6 this harlot is said to sit on a beast with seven
heads and ten horns. How does this relate to the description of
the dragon in chapter twelve (Rev. 12:3) and the sea-beast of
chapter thirteen? (Rev. 13:1)

This woman is arrayed in the garments of royalty and pros-
perity. How is this contrasted by the godly woman Paul
described in 1 Timothy 2:9, 10?

The woman's wealth is described by the "gold and precious
stones and pearls" with which she was adorned. Compare this
with Peter's admonition to godly women (1 Pet. 3:3).

How do the twin issues of immorality and idolatry, which
were called in the Old Testament "abominations to God"
(1 Kin. 14:22–24; 2 Kin. 21), help explain the name the mystery woman wore on her forehead?

How does this contrast with the name written on the foreheads of the 144,000 in Revelation 14:1?

What indicates that this "woman"—who is called "Baby-lon" and "the mother of harlots"—has been persecuting believers in Jesus Christ? (cf. Rev. 6:10; 16:5–6; 18:24)

In Rev. 17:7–11 the angel acknowledges to John the meanings behind the mystery (Rev. 17:7) of some of these symbols. He focuses on the beast which has seven heads and ten horns. This final beast empire represents all the previous seven beast empires, five of which had come and gone ("five have fallen"), "one is," and one was still to come in the future and would "continue for a short time."

What else do we know about this counterfeit Christ? List what you find in these verses:

- Ezek. 38:2, 14–17

- Dan. 11:36

- Matt. 24:15–21

- 2 Thess. 2:2–4, 9

- Rev. 12:13–7

- Rev. 13:3, 12

- Rev. 17:8

The ten horns in Revelation 17:12, 13 are said to represent the ten-nation federation which will give its power and strength to the beast (compare Dan. 7:23, 24 with Rev. 13:1). United, they will gather to make war with the Lamb, seeking to prevent Him from setting up His universal messianic kingdom (Rev. 19:19). Armageddon decides their awful fate.

The scarlet woman is both a religious system and a city (Rev. 17:18) which will "ride the beast" for a while. But finally, when the worship of the Beast is set in place (Rev. 13:4, 14, 15), the coalition of kings will resist her chokehold on their freedom and finances and react with vengeance.

What will they do to her? (See Rev. 17:16.)

How does this fit into God's plans? (v. 17)

THE FALL OF BABYLON THE GREAT
REVELATION 18:1–24

In Revelation 17 we see Babylon as a religious center, while in chapter 18 it is viewed in its social and commercial aspects. A godless government destroyed a Christless church in chapter 17, but in chapter 18 God Himself dethrones this godless government.

The first ten verses of Revelation 18 describe the fall of "Babylon the Great" from the perspective of the friends and allies who mourn its demise and destruction.

Verses 1–3 give several reasons for the fall of Babylon. List them:

Verses 4 and 5 contain a plea for God's people to "come out of her." God wants to protect His people as much as He wants to punish Babylon. What does this reference suggest to you regarding saints still in the world during this phase of the Tribulation period? Why?

Babylon is receiving a double portion of God's wrath in just retribution for her wrath against God's people (Rev. 18:6–8). How rapidly will this repayment be made when it is rendered? (vv. 8, 11)

It seems that many will mourn the succumbing of this great city (Rev. 18:9, 11, 15). Indicate how each of the following responded and are affected by Babylon's fall (18:9–20):

- The kings of the earth:

- The merchants of the earth:

- The shipmasters and sailors of the world:

- Heaven, along with the holy apostles and prophets:

BEHIND THE SCENES

"When the Book of Revelation was written, Babylon may have been a kind of code name for pre-Christian Rome that was built on seven hills (Rev. 17:9) and which was already persecuting the church. Since that time, generations of Christians have been able to identify their own Babylons and have found reassurance in Revelation's message."[2]

THE CHURCH EXULTS OVER THE JUDGMENT OF BABYLON
REVELATION 19:1–10

A great multitude in heaven (the "Church Triumphant") begins to rejoice over the fall of Babylon. Twice in this spontaneous expression of praise the word "Alleluia" is used. This word (which means "praise the Lord") occurs in the New Testament only in this particular passage of praise.

In Revelation 19:5 a voice comes from the throne admonishing the saints to praise the Lord. Then the great multitude responds and rejoices!

What is the basis of the blessing which is related in Revelation 19:9?

How should saints think of and relate to angels? (See Rev. 19:10; Col. 2:18; Heb. 1:13, 14.)

Revelation 19:7–9 relates the preparation of the bride of Christ for the Marriage Supper of the Lamb. The Bride's preparing her wedding apparel is also clearly presented in the parable of the wedding feast in Matthew 22:11–14.

 BIBLE EXTRA

It is interesting to note that in this same chapter, mention is made of two different suppers. The first is the Marriage Supper of the Lamb (Rev. 19:7–9). The other is a supper which God will prepare for the birds of the air to consume the carnage after the battle of Armageddon (vv. 17, 18) in the plain of Jezreel, east of Mount Carmel.

No wonder John was instructed to write: "Blessed are those who are called to the marriage supper of the Lamb" (Rev. 19:9).

CHRIST COMES ON A WHITE HORSE
REVELATION 19:11–16

The exciting Second Coming of Jesus Christ to Earth is recorded in the remainder of Revelation 19. The returning Savior's characteristics, companions, and conquests are given as the culmination toward which all of the Book of Revelation has been moving.

Jesus originally entered Jerusalem as the Messiah riding on a lowly donkey (Zech. 9:9; Matt. 21:1–11). This time He comes on a white horse, the symbol of conquest and victory!

What are the four names or titles mentioned in Revelation 19:11–16 for this Rider on a white horse?

He is also identified by his attributes, works, and companions. Record these below:

THE GREAT SUPPER OF GOD
REVELATION 19:17–19

As mentioned earlier, there are two different suppers indicated in this chapter. The first is the Marriage Supper of the Lamb (Rev. 19:7–9). The other is a supper which God will prepare for the fowls of the earth which fly in the midst of heaven (vv. 17, 18).

What is the purpose of this "great supper" prepared by God? (See v. 18.)

THE BEAST AND HIS ARMIES DEFEATED AT ARMAGEDDON
REVELATION 19:20, 21

The Rider on the white horse proceeds to deal first with members of the "Unholy Trinity." Name those who were "cast alive into the lake of fire burning with brimstone":

What does He do with the armies of the earth who had identified with those anti-Christ foes?

SATAN BOUND FOR 1,000 YEARS
REVELATION 20:1–3

What special restriction is reserved for Satan? (See Rev. 20:1–3.)

List the names which are used to identify the Evil One in verse 2.

How long is Satan to be bound? Why?

Why do you think he will again be released at the end of that time? (See 19:3; 20:7–10.)

 ### PROBING THE DEPTHS

"There are basically two broad positions regarding the reign of Christ during this 1,000-year period, or Millennium. The *premillennial view* holds that after the victory in Revelation 19, Christ will set up an earthly kingdom and will reign with the resurrected saints in peace and righteousness for 1,000 years, which may be a literal period or may be symbolic of an undetermined period. At the end of this period Satan will lead a final rebellion which will fail, and the world to come begins.

The *realized millennial view* (also called amillennial or present millennial) holds that the 1,000 years symbolize the period between the two advents of Christ, either as fully or progressively being realized. In this view, the millennial kingdom is a spiritual, not a political, reign of saints, being realized with Christ now, whether the believer is in heaven or on Earth."[3]

NOTE: The serious student will want to examine the eight charts illustrating various pre-, post- and a-millennial views shown on pages 1948–1951 of the *Spirit-Filled Life Bible*.

 FAITH ALIVE

While it is stimulating to study about the future reign of Christ with His saints here on earth, it is important to remember that He is **today** King of kings and Lord of lords.

Jesus taught his disciples that the "kingdom of God is within you" (Luke 17:21). As we walk with Him in obedience and holiness, His authority and anointing is transferred to us to transact His kingdom's business in His stead (Is. 61:1-3; Luke 4:18; John 1:16; 1 John 2:20, 27; 4:17). The full consummation of His kingdom awaits His literal, physical return. Until that time, let us serve Him using the "keys of the kingdom" He has granted us.

1. *Spirit-Filled Life Bible* (Nashville, TN: Thomas Nelson Publishers, 1991), 1984, "Word Wealth: Rev. 17:2, committed fornication."

2. "Babylon in the New Testament," *Nelson's Illustrated Bible Dictionary* (Nashville, TN: Thomas Nelson Publishers, 1986), 126.

3. *Spirit-Filled Life Bible*, 1989, notes on Revelation 20:1–8.

Lesson 13/ The Seven Sights
Revelation 20:4—22:21

In the sequence of John's visions, the 1,000-year millennial period sits like a peaceful valley between the last two great battles of the world: the campaign of Armageddon (Rev. 19:11–21) and the rebellion of Gog and Magog (Rev. 20:7–10). In this long-awaited setting the King consummates His rule and reign on earth.

THE SAINTS REIGN WITH CHRIST 1,000 YEARS
REVELATION 20:4–6

Who is specifically said to live and reign with Christ for this 1,000-year period?

Compare and contrast this promise with those given in Revelation 2:26–28; 3:12, 21; 12:11 and 1 Corinthians 6:2, 3.

What similarities can you see with the account of the "Ancient of Days" in Daniel 7:9, 22, and 27?

What term is used in Revelation 20:5 to describe this common experience for these saints?

When will the rest of the dead be resurrected to face judgment? (See 20:5, 6, 12–15; John 5:28, 29.)

What indicates that these resurrected believers will be rewarded with political and religious responsibilities?

THE RELEASE AND END OF THE ADVERSARY
REVELATION 20:7–10

From where do the "nations" come when Satan is allowed to deceive them upon his release from his millennial incarceration? (See Is. 66:18–23; Matt. 19:28; 25:31–46.)

 AT A GLANCE

Interpretations of Revelation 20:1–6[1]		
Postmillennial	Amillennial	Premillennial*
Christ will return *after* the 1,000 years. A golden age on the earth is ushered in by the triumph of the gospel through the church. The 1,000 years is viewed literally by some but symbolically by others.	There is *no* literal 1,000 years of Christ's reign on the earth. Christ is viewed as presently reigning either in: (1) the hearts of men, (2) heaven, or (3) the church. The 1,000 years is understood symbolically as representing an extended period of time.	The return of Christ will *precede* the establishment of His literal kingdom on earth Christ and His saints with Him will reign on the earth in fulfillment of O.T. and N.T. prophecy. The 1,000 years is understood as predicting a literal future reign of peace and righteousness on the earth.
*This view best explains ch. 20 and is the one affirmed in the study notes.		

What does Revelation 20:8b disclose about the population explosion during the Millennium?

 PROBING THE DEPTHS

"At the end of the 1,000 years, *Satan will be released* in the Earth again *to deceive.* It appears that many who submitted to Christ's rule during the Millennium did so without inner commitment to His lordship. The final deception of Satan separates these from those who have sincerely submitted. This is the last insurrection that the Lord will tolerate. Satan will next be *cast into the lake of fire and tormented . . . forever.*"[2]

Although Satan was condemned at the Cross, his final sentencing was stayed until our sovereign God was through using him for His own purposes. Now, after Armageddon, Satan is cast into "the lake of fire and brimstone." Compare this location with the place "prepared for the devil and his angels" in Matthew 25:41.

Who already inhabits the "lake of fire"? (See Rev. 19:20.)

When will the unsaved dead from all ages join them in this place of eternal torment? (See Luke 16:22–24; Rev. 20:11–15.)

If the beast and his armies are already destroyed (Rev. 19:19 ff.), who is Gog and Magog? (Rev. 19:8)

How extensive is the army of rebels Satan gathers to surround the "camp of the saints and the beloved city"?

What do we know of God's love for the city of Jerusalem? (See Ps. 78:68; 87:2.)

How does God deal with the rebels and with the devil who has deceived them?

THE GREAT WHITE THRONE JUDGMENT
REVELATION 20:11–15

This final judgment of the unbelieving dead is set in contrast to the Bema Seat Judgment of rewards which believers experienced (1 Cor. 3:13–15; 2 Cor. 5:9, 10).

How are the dead to be judged? (See Revelation 20:12, 13.)

Will there be degrees of punishment for unbelievers? (See Matt. 11:20–24.)

What is the ultimate destiny of those who are judged? (20:14–15)

HEAVEN AND EARTH RENOVATED
REVELATION 21:1–8

God originally created the earth and the heavenly atmosphere which surrounds it to be man's permanent home. He declared it "good" and delegated His rule over planet earth to man. But when man fell from his place of relationship with God he also forfeited his right to rule this earth.

Since that time "the whole creation groans and labors with birth pangs . . . until now" (Rom. 8:22) as Satan's destructive designs were multiplied. In Revelation 21, with Satan removed, God's redemption reaches even to His creation as He renovates both heaven and earth.

How may Peter's predictions (2 Pet. 3:10–13) point to this postmillennial event?

What indicates that the new earth will have a different environment as well? (Compare Rev. 21:1 with 22:1.)

Not only has God planned a *new environment* for his people, but also a *new experience of intimacy*. Previously, Paul explained that "we see in a mirror, dimly," but after "that which is perfect has come" we will see and relate "face to face" (1 Cor. 13:12). John explains (Rev. 21:3) that in the new earth God has chosen to "tabernacle" within us; to dwell with His creation in a new and intimate way.

Verse 4 indicates that citizens of the celestial kingdom will also have new emotions. What negative things will be no more? (See vv. 3, 4.)

The "overcomers" shall inherit all the "new" things mentioned in vv. 1–6. Review and summarize these here:

The glory of the overcomers is contrasted in verse 8 with the fate of the evil ones whose names were "not found in the Book of Life" and were cast into the lake of fire. What is this experience called? (See Rev. 21:8b.)

The New Jerusalem
Revelation 21:9—22:5

If the New Jerusalem is the bride of Christ, and if Christians are the inhabitants of that city, the scripture would be referring to the believers—the inhabitants of the New Jerusalem—as the bride of Christ. (Compare Revelation 21:2, 9, and 10.)

How did John describe the light which emanated from the Holy City?

Which precious stones or metals are mentioned as translucent and which as adornments?

What was unique about the construction of the wall, the gates, and the foundation of the city?

This New Jerusalem, the capital city of the "new heaven and new earth," is also unique for what is not there. This eternal state is distinguished from the millennial period by things which are missing. How many missing things can you find in the following verses of Revelation 21 and 22?

- 21:4

- 21:22

- 21:23; 22:5

- 21:25; 22:5

- 21:27

- 22:3

The first two verses of Revelation 22 tell about a river of life "proceeding from the throne of God and the Lamb." How does this compare to the water Jesus said he would give? (Compare John 7:37–39 and John 4:13, 14.)

The river is located right in the middle of a street in the new city. On each side of the riverbank is a special tree. What is it called?

Where do you recall reading about this tree in Scripture? (See Gen. 2:9; 3:22; Ezek. 47:12.)

What is unique about its fruit and leaves?

A Summary Exhortation
Revelation 22:6–19

In this final summary exhortation seven confirming witnesses testify to the authenticity of the message:[3]

1. God through His angel (Rev. 22:6)
2. John (Rev. 22:8, 9)
3. The witness of the angel (Rev. 22:10, 11)
4. The Lord Jesus (Rev. 22:12)
5. The Spirit (Rev. 22:17)
6. The bride
7. Him who hears

A Final Affirmation
Revelation 22:20, 21

Jesus reiterates His promise to return. It serves as a final assurance of that blessed hope.

Added to that hope, John reminds us of God's grace. It stands in sharp contrast to the wrath and judgments he has revealed in "the rest of the story."

 FAITH ALIVE

"Among the very last words of the Bible is this promise from the Lord Jesus, 'Surely I am coming quickly.' This blessed hope, which was declared by angels and spoken of by the apostles, is tenderly reiterated by the Lord at the very end of His Word. It is as if He wished to say, 'There is much in My Word that you need attend to, but do not let this hope be overshadowed: I am coming back soon.' Together with John, let us say, 'Even so, come, Lord Jesus!'"[4]

1. *The Believer's Study Bible* (Nashville, TN: Thomas Nelson Publishers, 1991), 1825, "Interpretations of Revelation 20:1–6."

2. *Spirit-Filled Life Bible* (Nashville, TN: Thomas Nelson Publishers, 1991), 1990, notes on Revelation 20:7–10.

3. Ibid., 1992, 1993, notes on Revelation 22:6–20.

4. Ibid., 1993, "Kingdom Dynamics: Rev. 22:20, Surely I Am Coming Quickly."